Maria Patricia Lewicki

Sustainability of the German Pension Scheme

Employment at Higher Ages and Incentives for Delayed Retirement

Sustainability of the German Pension Scheme

Employment at Higher Ages and
Incentives for Delayed Retirement

by
Maria Patricia Lewicki

KIT Scientific Publishing

Dissertation, Karlsruher Institut für Technologie (KIT)
Fakultät für Wirtschaftswissenschaften
Tag der mündlichen Prüfung: 28. Januar 2014
Referent: Prof. Dr. Berthold U. Wigger
Korreferent: Prof. Dr. J. Kowalski

Impressum

KIT Scientific Publishing

Karlsruher Institut für Technologie (KIT)
KIT Scientific Publishing
Straße am Forum 2
D-76131 Karlsruhe

KIT Scientific Publishing is a registered trademark of Karlsruhe Institute of Technology. Reprint using the book cover is not allowed.

www.ksp.kit.edu

Print on Demand 2014

ISBN 978-3-7315-0171-8
DOI: 10.5445/KSP/1000038392

Sustainability of the German Pension Scheme: Employment at Higher Ages and Incentives for Delayed Retirement

Zur Erlangung des akademischen Grades eines

Doktors der Wirtschaftswissenschaften

Dr. rer. pol.

von der Fakultät für Wirtschaftswissenschaften

des Karlsruher Instituts für Technologie (KIT)

genehmigte

DISSERTATION

von

Diplom-Wirtschaftsmathematikerin Maria Patricia Lewicki

Tag der mündlichen Prüfung:	28.01.2014
Referent:	Professor Dr. Berthold U. Wigger
Korreferent:	Professor Dr. Jan Kowalski

Karlsruhe 2014

Acknowledgement

First of all, I would like to thank my supervisor Professor Dr. Berthold U. Wigger who gave me the necessary support as well as the necessary freedom for my research project. I also owe many thanks to Professor Dr. Jan Kowalski, my second advisor and, further, Professor Dr. Martin Ruckes and Professor Dr. Hagen Lindstädt as members of the examination board.

This work uses data from the Research Data Centre of the German Centre of Gerontology (FDZ-DZA) as well as data from the Research Data Center of the German statutory pension insurance scheme (FDZ-RV). To both, I am grateful for providing access to data, which can be used by researchers like me with the purpose to broaden the knowledge of the economics of ageing.

I would like to thank all my colleagues, who accompanied me the last years in Karlsruhe. All of you somehow participated in this research project and made it a very pleasurable time.

I most deeply thank my sister, for all her encouragement and helpful advice, in any case and at any time. And last, I would like to thank Georg for all the love and happiness, he brings into my life.

Contents

List of Figures

List of Tables

Abbreviations

ADDR	adult disability dependency ratio
ADL	activities of daily living
AltEinkG	Alterseinkünftegesetz (law on old-age income)
AVmG	Altersvermögensgesetz (retirement savings act)
BMAS	Bundesministerium für Arbeit und Soziales (Federal Ministry of Labor and Social Affairs)
BMBF	Bundesministerium für Bildung und Forschung (Federal Ministry of Education and Research)
BMFSJ	Bundesministerium für Familie, Senioren, Frauen und Jugend (Federal Ministry of Family Affairs, Senior Citizens, Women and Youth)
DALYs	disability adjusted life years
DFLE	disability-free life expectancy
EIOPA	European Insurance and Occupational Pension Authority
EU	European Union
EU-SILC	European Union Statistics on Income and Living Conditions
FSO	Federal Statistical Office
GDP	gross domestic product
HALE	health-adjusted life expectancy
IADL	instrumental activities of daily living
KVdR	pensioners' health insurance
PAYGO	pay-as-you-go
POADR	prospective old-age dependency ratio
QALYs	quality adjusted life years
SEOP	German Socio-Economic Panel Study
US	United States of America
WHO	World Health Organization

1 Introduction

„Es gilt der Satz – zum Mitschreiben –: Die Rente ist sicher.“

(„It holds – for taking notes –: Social Security pensions are safe.“)[1]

(Dr. Norbert Blüm, 10.10.1997)[2]

1.1 Motivation

The aging society and threatening old-age poverty are two major political topics in Germany for the next decades. Handling these demographic challenges will be essential for Germany in order to remain one of the strongest economies in Europe. For this purpose a well-designed and sustainable pension scheme is necessary. Pension system design strongly depends on the society and the economy of the state.[3] Therefore, there is no optimal pension scheme, but, since societies and economies are permanently developing, also the pension schemes have to be reformed accordingly.

At the end of the 19th century, Germany is a pioneer in implementing social security systems. Still today, Germany takes a leading role among the welfare states of the European Union. At this time the pension schemes of the European states are various. Public pension schemes are mostly based on a pay-as-you-go (PAYGO) system, whereby current pensions are paid from current contributions. Several member states have additional occupational and/or private pension schemes. The latter can be mandatory or voluntary. Both are usually funded, in contrast to the unfunded public pension scheme. The importance of the different schemes varies across states. While most earning-related schemes are defined-benefit pensions, and thus are not linked directly to contributions but to benefits, minimum-guaranteed pensions are often offered,

---

[1] Own translation.

[2] 13/13198 Plenarprotokoll, Deutscher Bundestag – 13. Wahlperiode – 198. Sitzung, Bonn, p.17872.

[3] For a study of the normative and positive ramifications of public pension policies and economic growth see Wigger (2002).

which are usually means-tested. Further, not only old-age pensions are provided but also disability and survivors' pensions as well as early retirement pensions.[4]

Even though the pension schemes are diverse across Europe, all countries are facing the same challenges of the demographic change towards an older population. At the same time modern employment histories with a multitude of individual periods are changing the labor market and therefore also impacting the pension system. The *General Report on the Activities of the European Union - 2011* mentioned "reforming the pension system" as one of ten concrete priorities for 2011. In consequence, a new supervisory authority, the European Insurance and Occupational Pension Authority (EIOPA), was established and started operating in January 2011 with the aim of supporting the stability of the financial system, ensuring transparency of financial products, and markets and protecting all the parties in a pension scheme.[5] The limitation of the Authority to occupational pension schemes reflects the national authority for the public pension scheme of a certain state. Only a convergence of the statutory retirement ages has been discussed at a European level in order to overcome the upcoming challenges to the sustainability of the pension schemes. Still, in most European states, including Germany, the average retirement age is lower than the statutory retirement age. This is due to several possibilities of early retirement that are part of many pension schemes. Increasing the statutory retirement age from 65 to 67 and further abolishing different retirement ages for males and females might not be sufficient.[6] It seems obvious that, unless the pension systems are made sustainable in the long run, national budget balancing will be impossible. Nevertheless, a common efficient statutory retirement age might not be possible due to structural and social differences across Europe. Maybe a fixed retirement age would not be effective even at the national level? Thus, is it possible to overcome old structures and develop a modern pension scheme in Germany, which is flexible and sustainable at the same time? In the case of its success, it could then be a model for other industrial welfare states.

[4] For detailed information see European Commission (2009), p.28ff.

[5] See European Commission (2012a).

[6] For a detailed list of statutory retirement ages and recent reforms of the pension schemes see European Commission (2009).

Germany was the first country to establish a retirement scheme, which it did in 1889 under Otto von Bismarck. In the debate on 5 May 1884 about a renewal of the socialist laws Bismarck states:

"...geben Sie dem Arbeiter das Recht auf Arbeit, so lange er gesund ist, geben Sie ihm Arbeit, so lange er gesund ist, sichern Sie ihm Pflege, wenn er krank ist, sichern Sie ihm Versorgung ,wenn er alt ist..."[7]

("...give the worker the right to work as long as he is healthy, give him work as long as he is healthy, assure him care if he is ill, assure him provision when he is old...")[8]

The question is: at which specific age is a person old? At that time only individuals aged 70 were eligible for retirement. Around 1900 the average life expectancy of newborns was about 45 years.[9] Further, the share of persons within the German population above the age of 70 was only 2.8%.[10] In 2011 this share was almost 16% if one includes individuals aged 65 – 69 the share was 21%.[11] The Federal Statistical Office (FSO) forecasts an ongoing increase with a share of up to 32% in 2030.[12] Such an increase of retirees affects negatively for the financial stability of the pension scheme, since fewer employees are paying contributions and more pensions entitlements have to be paid to the retirees. At the same time the total duration of individual employment decreases. In the past only a small number of individuals had access to higher education. Therefore, the majority entered the labor force at a younger age leading to longer employment periods.[13] After decreasing the statutory retirement age to 65 in 1916, recently, due to the demographic changes, the statutory retirement age has been raised again by two

[7] Berlin (1884), p. 6.

[8] Own translation.

[9] See Statistisches Bundesamt (2012a), p. 19ff.

[10] Data from Federal Statistical Office.

[11] Data from Federal Statistical Office.

[12] See Statistisches Bundesamt (2009), p. 17.

[13] The increase in the age of individuals entering the labor force can be observed for all education classes (see Konietzka (2010), p. 165 or Trischler (2011), p. 41). However, a reverse tendency can be predicted for the coming years due to the abolishment of the compulsory military service, a shortening of the schooling years of the secondary school, a shortening of the years of study, and open apprenticeship positions.

years from 65 to 67. This reform was unpopular and widely criticized by the labor unions, although the absolute number of years in retirement is still high because of the increasing life expectancy. Is employment only seen as an obligation and a burden? Are not the elderly willing to stay longer in employment because of social contacts, intellectual stimulation, and having fun?

There exist already various studies on the German pension system. Many of them have analyzed the topic of early retirement by discussing actuarial fair or neutral deductions, i.e., efficient cuts of pension entitlements in the case of early drawing of the pension. Also the right balance between the three pillars, public, occupational and private pensions, has been studied widely in the literature. It has often been claimed that the elderly are retiring too early and saving too little themselves. So far comparatively few attempts have been made to do research on the elderly after retirement. As long as people are getting older, it is crucial to know about the way of life of the elderly, their needs, potentials and motives. The existing literature shows a huge lack of analysis of the incentives for employment at higher ages, especially after retirement. Further, previous research has neglected to differentiate empirically between early and delayed retirement. This thesis aims to contribute to the research in the field of retirement by filling the observed gaps in the literature on delayed retirement and on the incentives for employment at higher ages.

1. **What determines delayed retirement? Why is this phenomenon so rare?**

2. **What could be the right incentives for fostering employment at higher ages? How does the pension scheme have to be reformed to adapt to the changes in the biographies of future cohorts? How can it be designed to become more flexible without losing sustainability?**

Both research questions will be answered in this thesis using a theoretical and an empirical perspective. The main focus is on the sustainability of old-age provision within the German public pension scheme in the long run. Based on the discussion of relevant trends in demography and the labor market, a modern, more flexible approach to a public pension system is proposed.

1.2 Outline of the thesis

The thesis is divided into six chapters, which are outlined in the following.

Chapter 2 discusses the upcoming economic challenges in an aging society. On the basis of the current state of research, this chapter describes these current demographic as well as economic developments in Germany. Prospective trends are included which cover three relevant fields: life expectancy and fertility, pension system design and modern employment biographies. All three fields directly impact the pension scheme. Recent developments, trends, and problems that may arise from the demographic change will be elaborated for each field. Moreover, current statistics and empirical results are discussed with the intention of attaining a more in-depth knowledge of the retirement situation in Germany in particular.

The findings of the previous chapter are used in **chapter 3** to analyze the adaptiveness of the German pension system. For all three relevant fields mentioned potential approaches are considered. Considering the life expectancy, it is necessary to distinguish between healthy years of life and years where the individual's life is impacted by illness or disability. A brief insight into public health is provided in order to be able to evaluate the ability to work at higher ages. Germany is not the only country to cope with an aging society. Other states are facing similar challenges: thus selected international pension systems and their efforts to cope with them are presented. In doing so, the German pension scheme can be ranked and evaluated on an international scale. Further, potentials for improvement are revealed. The last section of this chapter focuses on the labor market. Public as well as private campaigns are listed in order to evaluate the capability of the labor market to handle the upcoming structural changes in the labor force.

Chapter 4 answers my first research question empirically. Using a multiple logistic regression, the determinants of early and deferred retirement are analyzed and contrasted to regular retirement. For both options, early retirement and deferred retirement, determining factors are identified and discussed. The aim of this chapter is to consider the determinants of early and deferred retirement in a unified framework. The underlying idea is that the same factors that determine early retirement also determine deferred retirement, but with the opposite sign. If this is the case, the lessons that can be drawn from the evidence on early retirement, can contribute to an understanding of how to encourage individuals to work longer. In doing so, an essential research gap in regard to delayed retirement will be filled. Further, these results contribute to the analysis in the following chapter, which answers my second research question.

In **chapter 5** I propose a modification of the German pension scheme. This new pension scheme does without a fixed pension eligibility age but instead uses strong incentives to work at higher ages due to age-specific earning points. Using data from the German public pension insurance a markov decision process is modeled to show the feasibility of the alternative pension scheme. Four different modifications are chosen, which differ in the progression of the weighting. The upcoming effects and the impact on the sustainability of the pension scheme are presented and discussed. As a result of the implemented modifications, a higher efficiency of the public pension scheme is attained in the long run.

Finally, **chapter 6** summarizes the findings and gives answer to both research questions. Moreover, some policy recommendations are offered and further initiatives are proposed.

2 Economic challenges in an aging society

Medical progress, expanding knowledge, healthy living and various other aspects have led to an increasing life expectancy of individuals in many European countries, including Germany. Contemporaneously, decreasing fertility rates occur due to the increasing autonomy of women and changes in social cohesion and the modern way of life. Both influence the age structure of the population and shift the skewness of the age distribution towards the elderly. Pension reforms are necessary to handle these movements adequately in order to avoid the bankruptcy of the pension system. In addition, modern employment biographies show an increasing number of different periods and even simultaneous states, so that individual employment histories are becoming more complex. Not only will working at higher ages be more important in the future but also the demand will rise. The labor market has to adapt to these desired effects. It is especially difficult to address these economic challenges effectively because no society has experienced such an age transition before. So there is no country to learn from. Instead, countries like Germany will serve as pioneers in this area.

2.1 Increasing life expectancy and declining fertility rates

The global age transition began around 1950. In many industrialized countries there was a baby boom. Also families in the developing world became bigger due to the decline in child mortality. Thus, in the following years the working age population, i.e. individuals between 25 and 59, increased and outnumbered the children and the elderly. In the future, increasing life expectancy will boost the population of the elderly, whereas decreasing fertility rates will downsize the child population. The absolute number of the elderly will rise. Never before in human history, was the share of the elderly larger in many populations. Of course, there exist national differences. While most Asian and African countries are quite at the beginning of the age transition, higher income societies like the US, Europe and East Asia will face these challenges soon.

Focusing on the national level, statistical evidence can be found that Germany is experiencing this age transition. Several aspects, including life expectancy and fertility rates, affect the demographic change within the German population. At first sight, it might seem contradictory that the number of deaths will increase in the future after being quite constant at around 840 000 per year since 2001. This increase is not caused by a spread of diseases or by the deterioration of medical care. Rather, the changes in age structure determine this fact. An increasing life expectancy leads to more individuals reaching higher ages. Already today, half of deceased individuals are over 80. Further, the large cohorts of 1930 are getting old. Therefore, the number of deaths is supposed to rise to one million in 2030.[14]

An individual's life expectancy is not constant over time but only valid at the moment it was calculated. It is a prediction based on an empirical model, about how long an individual will survive from a certain point in time. Often, this certain point in time is the date of birth, but also the time of retirement is used in order to estimate the remaining time in retirement. The basis for an analysis of life expectancy was set during the German Reich by the FSO's creation of the first periodic mortality table of 1871/1881. The FSO estimates on an ongoing basis life expectancy in Germany based on periodic mortality tables and publishes them annually.[15] The tables differentiate between males and females because there are significant differences in mortality rates between these groups.[16] Periodic life expectancy tables show the current probability of death for individuals of different ages in the current year. Thus, specific mortality characteristics of a certain period, e.g., a flu epidemic, are represented in the table. The estimated life expectancies in this table equal the average number of remaining years of individuals with a certain age. This number is conditional on the specific mortality characteristic valid during this period. Future changes are not considered. Besides periodic mortality tables also cohort mortality tables exist. They show, in contrast, the probability of death

[14] See Statistische Ämter des Bundes und der Länder (2011), p. 13.

[15] For a detailed description of the method used and an historical overview see Eisenmenger and Emmerling (2011). For an example see Statistisches Bundesamt (2012b).

[16] From the middle of the 18th century women have had a higher life expectancy than men (see Kalben (2000) and Waldron (1985)). Reasons for that have their roots in biological aspects but also the way of life and the use of health care are important factors (see Oksuzyan et al. (2008)).

of individuals from a given cohort over the course of their lifetime. Such a study requires a complete examination of all years and individuals and is therefore a very complex method. For the estimations, all members of a cohort must have passed away, which requires an observation period of more than 100 years. Moreover, territorial changes, migration or wars imperil the integrity of the sample.[17]

Although the periodic mortality tables are rather simple to calculate, they have one specific drawback. For the approximation of the average life expectancy of a population mortality rates are supposed to remain constant over the whole evaluation period. Oeppen and Vaupel (2002) have shown that, worldwide, living conditions and mortality rates have changed rapidly in the past 160 years. Moreover, they are almost certain to do so in the future. As a result, life expectancy for the German population is underestimated.[18]

Besides the estimation of life expectancies, mortality tables include survival probabilities, i.e., the probability of dying between two points in time. Bongaarts and Feeney (1998) have pointed to the *tempo effect* that causes distortion of survival probabilities when the average age at childbearing respectively at death changes. Some attempts at alternative tempo-adjusted mortality rates have been made, but no satisfactory solution has been found so far.[19]

For a more precise calculation of life expectancy an accurate assumption about the development of future survival probabilities is needed. Several methods match historical data more accurately than periodic mortality tables do. The most common method has been proposed by Lee and Carter (1992). Ever since, several modifications have been made.[20] Using their method Lee and Carter provide mortality tables that closely fit the real mortality patterns in the United States between 1933 and 1987. This

---

[17] See Statistisches Bundesamt (2012c).

[18] For example, according to the periodic mortality table of the Federal Statistical Office for the period between 1901 and 1910 the estimated average life expectancy for females at birth was 48.33 years. In contrast, referring to the equivalent cohort mortality tables, the average life expectancy for women was 52.5 years in 1900 and increased steadily to 58.83 years in 1910.

[19] See Luy (2010).

[20] For an overview see Lee (2000).

method is currently used for the official mortality tables in the US and long run forecasts of life expectancy by the U.S. Census Bureau.

As mentioned before, life expectancies for women are higher than for men. This holds for almost every period and every country. Luy (2011) has demonstrated in a "Cloister Study" that this gender gap is mainly determined by the risk-taking behavior of the men and only to a limited extent by biological reasons. In addition to gender, several living conditions influence life expectancy. The living conditions of the mother already have an impact in the utero and therefore on the future human being. The mother's malnutrition and poor health care are important factors for shorter life spans (see for example Van den Berg et al. (2008) or Doblhammer and Vaupel (2001)). Further, smoking cigarettes or consuming alcohol during pregnancy increases the risk of stillbirth (see for example Aliyu (2008)), growth retardation, and a higher prevalence of diverse diseases and disorders (see for example Gilliland (2001) or Hannigan and Armant (2000)). Although the overall effects have not yet been quantified and some disagreement among researchers still exists, these conditions are likely to decrease life expectancy.[21]

During an individual's life time multiple aspects affect life expectancy. Obviously, overall health is a deciding factor. In 2010 the most common causes of death in Germany were cardiovascular diseases (41.1%), various kinds of cancer (25.5%), and diseases of the respiratory system (7.0%).[22] The public health care system is therefore an essential factor in healing and preventing illnesses and supporting a longer lifespan.

A higher level of education affects life expectancy in a positive way, which is confirmed by several studies like Becker (1998), Reil-Held (2000) and Kroll and Lampert (2009).

Mortality risk decreases immediately after marriage for both women and men, whereas for the latter the effect is stronger. A higher mortality risk right after divorce is only a short-term effect. These gains in life expectancy due to marriage can be explained

---

[21] See Bakker et al. (2010).

[22] See Statistisches Bundesamt (2010), p.1.

partly by a selection bias on the marriage market.[23] Perceived family support also raises life expectancy.[24]

By analyzing data from the statutory pension insurance Scholz and Schulz (2009) have examined the positive effect of employment on life expectancy. Generally, physical activity increases life expectancy. A literature overview on this specific correlation is given by Reimers et al. (2012).

Overall, a variety of factors influence the average life expectancy. Extensive research confirms many of these interdependencies. However, what holds on average for a population does not need to hold for a certain individual. A Danish study confirms that the average life expectancy for smokers is significantly lower than for non-smokers.[25] At the same time, Christian Mortensen, born in Denmark in 1882, reached an age of 115 and was the oldest human alive at the time of the study. Throughout most of his life, he smoked cigars regularly and recommended them for a long life.[26]

The first available reliable data on life expectancy in Germany is for the period 1871 till 1881. At that time, the average life expectancy at birth was 35.58 years for men and 38.45 years for women. The total population count was 41 million in 1871.[27] From then on, the average life expectancy increased steadily and doubled to 77.72 years for men and 82.73 years for women in the period between 2009 and 2011.[28] Figure 1 visualizes the increase of average life expectancy at birth in Germany since 1871.

---

[23] See Brockmann and Klein (2004).

[24] See Ross and Mirowsky (2002).

[25] See Bronnum-Hansen and Juel (2001).

[26] See Wilmoth et al. (1996).

[27] See Hubert (1998), p. 330.

[28] See Statistisches Bundesamt (2012b).

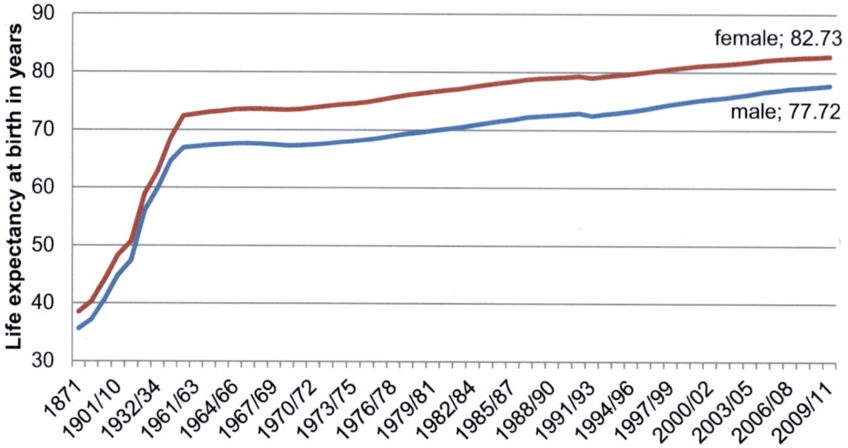

Note: Before 1960 irregular data, from 1960 annually collected data. Source: Federal Statistical Office; own illustration.

Figure 1: Life expectancy at birth in Germany

A long-term perspective of statistical data from the FSO reveals that the average life expectancy for both genders has increased about three months per year at a nearly linear rate over the last 140 years until 2010. Similar findings are stated by Oeppen and Vaupel (2002). This trend is ongoing: comparing the last two periodic mortality tables from 2008/2010 and 2009/2011, the gain in life expectancy for newborn males is three months and for newborn females is two months. Also the life expectancy of the elderly rises: females aged 65 gain a surplus in their further life expectancy of two months, whereas males aged 65 gain one month. This continuing augmentation seems without limit.[29] Oeppen and Vaupel have demonstrated that every published estimate of the maximum life expectancy has been broken just a few years after its prediction.

[29] See Wilmoth (2000).

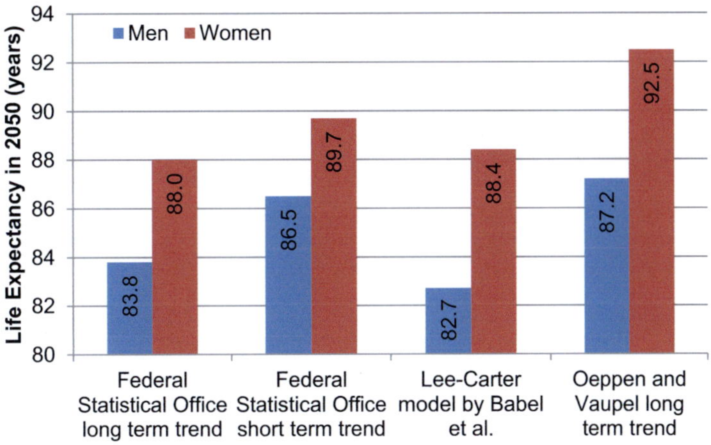

Source: own illustration.

Figure 2: Life expectancy forecasts for Germany

As can be seen from Figure 2, life expectancy forecasts for 2050 differ apparently among different projections. The FSO models two scenarios; a short term trend based on data since 1970 and a long term trend based on data since 1871. As mentioned before, the method used by the FSO does not allow for any changes in mortality rates during the projection period. The Lee-Carter model, on the other hand, does. Within the fitting process of this model any mitigating or boosting effects are considered as leading to a more accurate projection. Oppen and Vaupel predict the highest life expectancy by assuming a rate of increase of 90 days per year under ideal circumstances.

The population balance results from the difference between the number of births and the number of deaths. Between 1991 and 2008 this balance was negative: therefore, each year more persons died than were born, the deficit fluctuating between 50,000 in 1997 and 160,000 in 2008. This deficit is supposed to rise because of decreasing fertility rates and increasing numbers of deaths. Forecasts for 2030 indicate a negative population balance of 410,000.[30]

Migration changes the population, especially the age structure. While emigration is quite stable over time, immigration shows a high fluctuation. Individuals immigrating to Germany are generally younger than individuals emigrating. Hence, migration mitigates

[30] See Statistische Ämter des Bundes und der Länder (2011), p. 15.

the aging of the population. The FSO assumes the migration balance to be positive and to increase slightly in the middle and long term. The increase emerges from the decline in the potential labor force due to the aging population as well as from increased worldwide migration due to climate change. From 2014 on the balance should remain on a level of 100 000.[31]

The cumulative effect of all aspects described in the previous paragraphs is a decline of the German population. As can be seen from Table 1, the population counted 82.0 million in 2008, with a downward trend expected, leading to a projected 77.4 million in 2030.

2008	2015	2020	2025	2030
82.0	80.8	79.9	78.8	77.4

Note: in millions, from 2015 based on projections of the FSO

Table 1: German population

The population's age structure has faced huge changes over the last decades and will also continue changing in the future. A population pyramid visualizes these changes very well (see Figure 3). At the end of 1910 the age structure was really a pyramid. Just 40 years later a pyramid is identified only with difficulty. In 2008 the shape of the age structure has absolutely nothing in common with a pyramid. Persons aged 65 and older make up 20% of the total population. The population aged between 20 and 65 is in general seen as the potential labor force and makes up 61%. The group of persons below 20 counts for 19% of the population and is already a bit smaller than the group of persons aged 65+. Based on the forecasts this gap will grow in future. Thus the group of the elderly (65+) will reach a share of 29%, whereas the share of persons below 20 will decline to 17% in 2030.[32]

[31] See Statistische Ämter des Bundes und der Länder (2011), p. 18.

[32] See Statistische Ämter des Bundes und der Länder (2011), p. 23f.

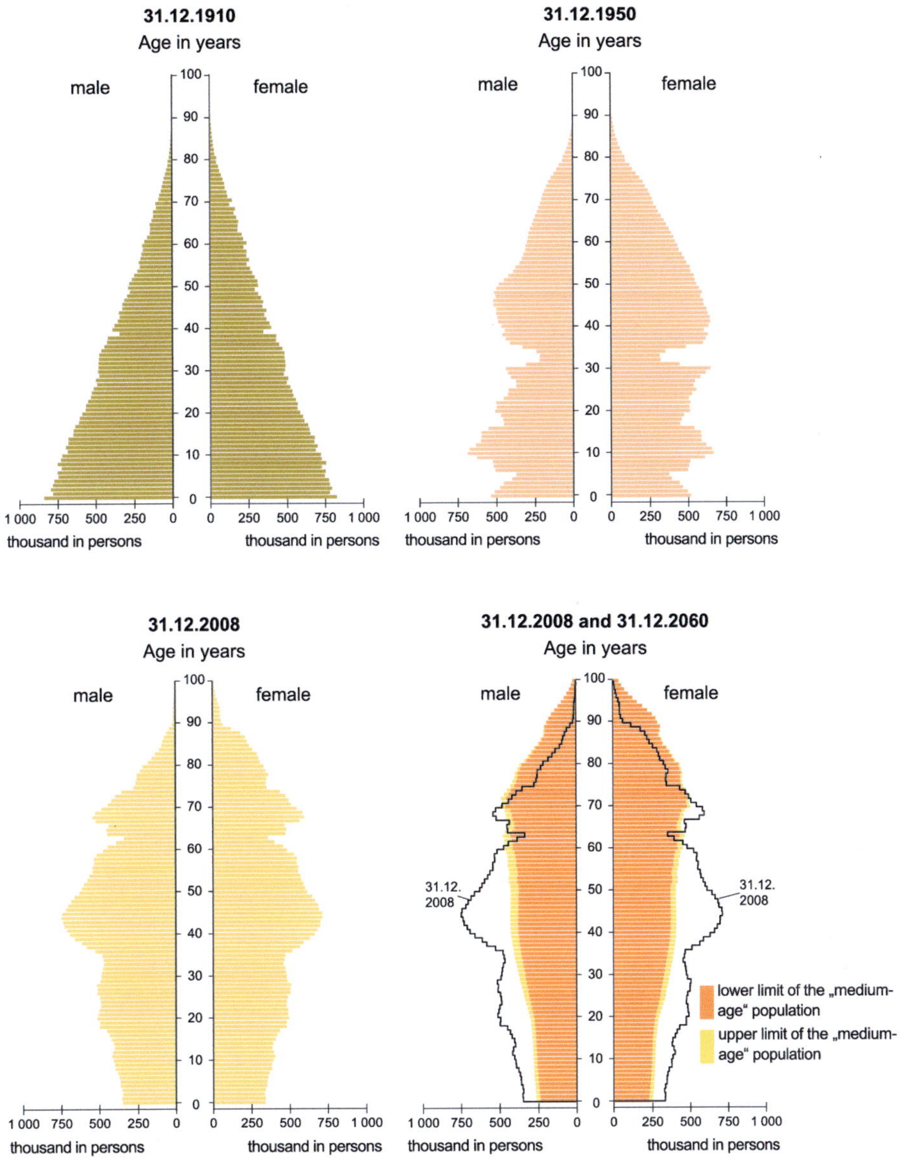

Source: Statistisches Bundesamt (2009), p.15; own translation.

Figure 3: Population pyramids for Germany

The decline in the fertility rate over the last decades is one essential reason for the changing age structure of the population. Fewer newborns narrow the base of the pyramid. Figure 4 depicts the number of births over time. The peak was reached in 1964 just in the middle of the baby-boom. In the following decades the number declined due to changes in the family and social structure and the availability of the birth-control pill. The number of births strongly depends on the number of women of childbearing age, which is, from a statistical view, between 15 and 49. Since 1998 this number has also been declining (see Figure 5). In line with the declining fertility rates this number will continue to fall in the future.[33]

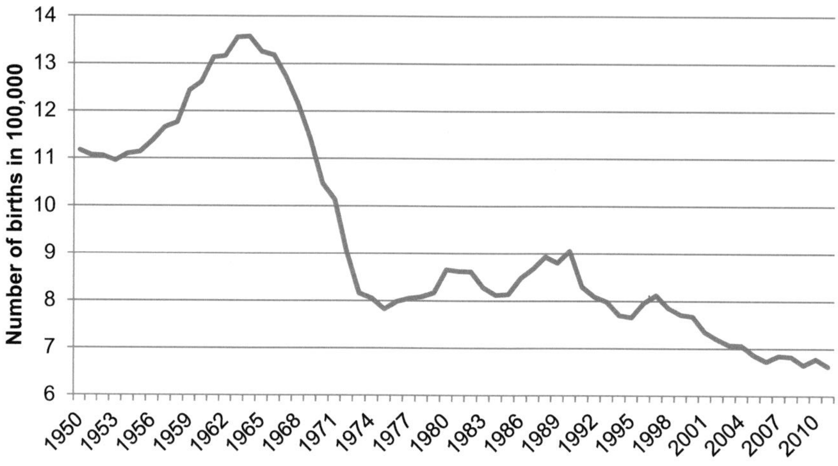

Source: German Federal Statistical Office; own illustration.

Figure 4: Number of births in Germany over time

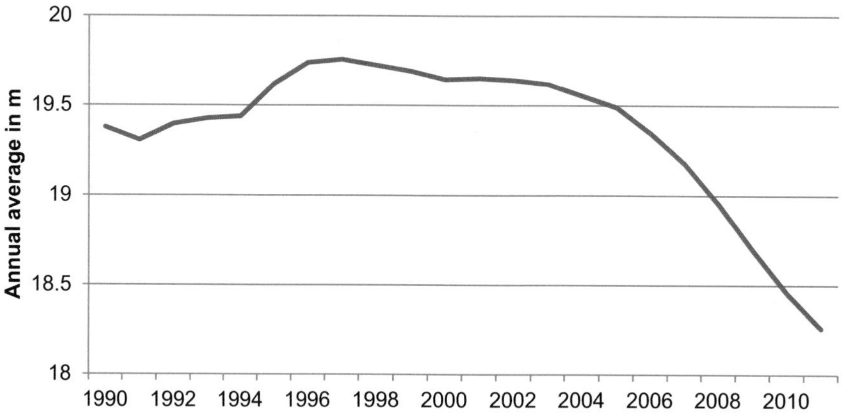

Source: German Federal Statistical Office; own illustration.

Figure 5: Number of women in Germany aged between 15 and 49

The older a woman is when giving birth to her first child, the shorter the period of life in which she is able to give birth to more children. This age is going up, especially for more highly educated women because of longer education phases and the focus on their own

[33] See Statistisches Bundesamt (2012d).

careers.[34] As a result, a future decline in the total number of births may be anticipated. So far, over the last 20 years, the average number of children per German woman did not change significantly and is consistent low at 1.3. Foreign women are often honored for a higher number of children. In the beginning of the 90s immigrant women give birth to two children on average. In succeeding years they seem to have conformed more strongly to the behavior of German women and have decreased the average number of children to 1.6 in 2010. Likewise the average number of children per mother has not changed remarkably since 1940 and stagnates at about two. Notwithstanding, the share of childless women within the society has increased. This tendency is rather unlikely to reverse in future since simultaneously the number of married women decreases and with it the probability of having a baby at all. Another tendency influencing fertility in a negative way is the higher education of women. The higher the education of the woman, the lower the number of children she has. Mothers having more than two children are strongly represented at the lowest educational level.[35]

To conclude this section, the demographic development reflects the tendencies towards increasing life expectancy and low fertility rates. Thus, there is a necessity to accept these trends and make use of the potential of the elderly, since this group will represent a large share of the population in the foreseeable future.

2.2 Pension reforms

From 2005 on, the OECD has published "Pension at a Glance" every two years as a guideline for all OECD and G20 countries. This publication provides indicators on retirement systems as well as policy recommendations and caveats with regard to demographic and economic challenges. Further, in 2012 the "OECD Pension Outlook 2012"[36] was published, including a special focus on the financial crisis and private

---

[34] In 1965 the average woman's age at the time of her first childbirth was 23.2; in 2010 it was 27.4 (see Statistisches Bundesamt (2012c)).

[35] See Statistisches Bundesamt (2012c).

[36] See OECD (2012a).

pensions. In this edition, as already in the 2009 edition of "Pensions at a Glance", six objectives of retirement income provision were stated:[37]

1. pension system's coverage (including mandatory and voluntary schemes)
2. adequacy of retirement benefits
3. affordability of pensions to contributors and taxpayers and financial sustainability
4. work incentives, i.e., achieve minimal distortions in labor supply
5. minimizing administrative costs
6. security of benefits through diversification of retirement savings

Obviously, to some extent, these objectives interact with each other. The aim of a sustainable pension system design is to cope this trade-offs in a best way.

The German statutory public pension system was established in 1889 as the first retirement system worldwide, starting providing pensions from the age of 70 for workers at a very low contribution rate of 1.7%. From then on, several reforms have been made. A selection of the most important ones is highlighted in the following.

Widow's and orphan's pensions were established in 1912. A special pension for unemployed persons aged 60 followed in 1929. Earlier, in 1916, the statutory retirement age was lowered to 65. The health insurance for retirees (KVdR) was introduced in 1941/42. In the following years the contribution rate rose gradually up to 5.6% in 1949. Within the same year a major increase, almost doubling the contribution rate, took place. Then, the contribution rate was 10.0%, the rate gradually rising over the next decades. A major pension reform took place in 1957/58, when a dynamic retirement formula was introduced and pensions were adjusted to the development of gross earnings. The transformation towards a pure PAYGO system took place in 1968/69 with a capital reserve of three monthly expenditures. This capital reserve had the purpose of compensating for fluctuations in contributions during the period as well as economic fluctuations and was, from 1977 on, therefore named fluctuation reserve. Over the years more and more groups of employees were covered by the public pension system. With the reform in 1972 the public pension system opened access to

[37] A similar list of objectives is also stated by the World Bank (see Holzmann and Hinz (2005)).

all citizens. Additionally, a special pension for long-standing insurant from the age of 63, a pension for severely handicapped persons as well as a pension due to limited earning capacity from the age of 62 were established. Further, a flexible retirement in the form of early retirement was allowed. The discrimination of women was eliminated in 1985 by taking periods of child care into account. At the beginning of the 90s the politicians realized that the previous expansions of benefits threatened the financial stability of the pension system. They enacted the pension reform act '92, which included several cuts to the generosity of the plan. From 1992 onwards, pensions were adjusted to the development of net earnings. Simultaneously, all pensionable ages were increased. Further, for each month of earlier retirement a deduction of 0.3% has to be accepted. In 1995 the compulsory long-term care insurance was introduced to which retirees also have to pay partial contributions. One year later, in 1996, more cuts through new acts followed. Thus, for example, the credited periods for education were shortened to 3 years. These limitations were not efficient enough, so the pension reform act '99 was passed in 1997. The objective was to decrease future pension levels. For that reason a demographic factor that makes the pension level depend on life expectancy was added to the pension formula. Right after the federal election in 1998, this factor was suspended before it even came into practice.

Since the German statutory public pension system consists of only a single tier, the federal government made a great effort to encourage voluntary private pensions. As a result, in 2001 the Altersvermögensgesetz (AVmG)[38], i.e., a retirement savings act, was enacted to foster a voluntary and funded private pension, the "Riester-Rente", through tax reliefs with the aim of closing future deficits in the PAYGO system. An amendment act[39] included a corresponding "Riester"-factor to the retirement formula in order to lower the pension payments because of the higher responsibility of the individuals to save privately. In the following years, the fluctuation reserve was decreased gradually to finally 32% of a monthly expenditure in 2004 and from this year on has been renamed as sustainability reserve. In contrast, the contribution rate reached 19.5% in 2004. In

[38] Altersvermögensgesetz (AVmG): Act reforming the public pension insurance and on subsidizing a funded old-age asset (06/2001 – BGB1. I S. 1310) valid from 01/2002.

[39] Altersvermögensergänzungsgesetz (AVmEG): Amendment of AVmG (13/2001 – BGB1. I S. 403) valid from 01/2002.

order to avoid further augmentations, the pension adjustments were deferred temporarily. Further, retirees have to pay full contributions to the compulsory long-term care insurance. In 2004 the Alterseinkünftegesetz (AltEinkG)[40], i.e., law on old-age income, changed the upstream taxation to a downstream taxation allowing for a transition period till 2040. That means that prior to retirement all contributions to the pension insurance are free of personal income taxation. In return, pension income has to be fully taxed after retirement. At the same time, the RV – Nachhaltigkeitsgesetz, i.e., pension insurance sustainability act, came into force. In line with the pension adjustment in July 2005, a sustainability factor modified the pension formula with a damping effect to stabilize the contribution rate in the long run. This factor takes account of the ratio between contributors and retirees and decreases the pension level correspondingly. The last substantial reform occurred in 2007, as the statutory retirement age was raised to 67. The transition period started in 2012 and increases the pensionable age stepwise by two months per year. From 2029 on the statutory retirement age will be 67 for all insurants. Further, from 2007 the contribution rate was set to 19.9% and was lowered slightly to 19.6% in 2012.

On the whole, the overall impression is that the reforms have been beneficial for the financial stability of the German pension system. The attempts described to adjust pensions to the demographic change seem effective, primarily in the short-run. As a result of the latest reforms and the overall positive economic trend, the sustainability reserve has an explicit surplus of 1.41 monthly expenditures reaching almost the maximum of 1.5.[41] Despite the forecasts of increasing pension claims resulting from the ongoing demographic change, future savings for expenditures are not intended within a PAYGO system. Moreover, if the reserve exceeds one and a half monthly expenditures, as will be the case, the contribution rate has to be decreased by law. Thus, the Federal Government decreased the contribution rate by 0.7% to 18.9% to the beginning of 2013.

[40] Alterseinkünftegesetz (AltEinkG): Act on realignment of the personal income taxation of retirement provisions and old-age pensions (07/2004 – BGB1. I S. 1427) valid from 01/2005.

[41] The sustainability reserve is legally allowed to range between 0.2 and 1.5 monthly expenditures of the pension insurance (§§ 216, 217, SGB VI).

In respect of the objectives proposed by the OECD, the reforms of the German pension system can be compared with them, in order to check the extent of fulfillment. This evaluation is presented in Table 2. Concerning coverage, adequacy, and work incentives, Germany has implemented corresponding reforms and improved fulfillment in these categories. But there are still some open topics, like a mandatory pension for the self-employed or threatening old-age poverty. Further, there are some potential improvements in the fields of sustainability, administrative efficiency (regarding private pensions), and security because of a low diversification.

In Germany nearly 80% of old-age income derives from public pensions, while private pensions account for less than 5%.[42] The attempts to foster an additional third tier of voluntary private pensions have been only partially effective as Schröder (2011) has demonstrated in a study. Only one third of all qualified persons concluded a contract by 2011, the participation rate being especially low in households with lower income. Further, the rates of returns are predicted to be low. Therefore, it is uncertain if the future pension gap, i.e., the difference in pension amount between the pension level prior to the reforms and after the reforms, will be closed sufficiently to avoid old-age poverty.

[42] See OECD (2012a), p.23.

	Objectives	Measures	Comments	OECD's evaluation[43]
1	Coverage	Insurance opened to all citizens, women's equality, tax incentives for private pensions (AVmG)	A mandatory pension for self-employed is still open to debate.	Corresponding reforms were implemented.
2	Adequacy	Indexation, adjusting contribution rates	Threatening old-age poverty still remains.	Corresponding reforms were implemented.
3	Sustainability	Sustainability factor, Riester factor	Pension reductions are limited to prevent strong declines.	
4	Work incentives	Increasing retirement ages	Age increase does not compensate increase in life expectancy.	Corresponding reforms were implemented.
5	Administrative efficiency		Private pensions still not widespread, high administrative costs, low rate of return.	
6	Security		Low diversification	

Table 2: Objectives of retirement income provisions – evaluation of Germany

Conspicuously, most reforms tackle the problem directly by cutting pension benefits or increasing pensionable ages. Even if the effectiveness is quite high, such reforms are generally unpopular in the society, i.e., to the voters. Therefore, they are only difficult to implement. The intuitive option of linking the retirement age directly to the life expectancy, as was recommended by the German Council of Economic Experts, would lead to a retirement age of 68 in 2045 and of 69 in 2060.[44] Getting sufficient political support for this option seems rather unlikely. Another, more indirect way, is to initiate reforms in the labor market to support employment at higher ages. Currently, retirees

[43] The OECD evaluates reforms between the start of the crisis in September 2007 and February 2012.

[44] See Sachverständigenrat (2011), p. 196.

who have reached the statutory retirement age can be employed and are not subjected to any earning limits. Moreover, they are exempt from some social contributions, in particular contributions to unemployment insurance and to pension insurance.[45] This implies a higher net income: in 2012 both contribution rates added up to 22.6%. On the other hand, while drawing early pension certain earning limits have to be considered. Earnings include the monthly gross income, the monthly taxed-based profits as well as similar income. Depending on the amount of earnings the pension will be paid fully or partially. In the latter case, the pension is graded at a two-third, a half, or a one-third partial pension. The earning limits for partial pensions are calculated individually based on the salary of the last three years before retirement and the region (i.e. eastern or western Germany) where the earnings were made. Twice a year, it is permitted to exceed the limit up to double the amount. When drawing a full pension, a monthly earnings limit of 400€ has to be adhered to.

Gasche and Krolage (2011) point out that the grading of pensions implies strong disincentives. Marginal costs near the limits of two grades exceed 100%, so that increasing earnings can even lead to a reduction of the total income. The regulations of individual earning limits are complicated anyway. Thus, a flexible transition from employment into retirement is not provided. Statistical data from the German pension insurance shows that at the end of 2011 only a marginal fraction of 0.0013% of all old-age pensions were drawn as partial pensions.[46] Thus, does the society desire the transition to be flexible at all?

2.3 Modern employment biographies

In addition to the demographic change also new trends concerning employment biographies can be observed. On the one hand the employment rate of women is still

[45] The omission applies only to employees: i.e. employers still have to pay their part of these contributions.

[46] See Deutsche Rentenversicherung Bund (2012), p. 25.

rising. On the other hand the rate of atypical employment[47] is also rising. Both trends can be seen in Figure 6.

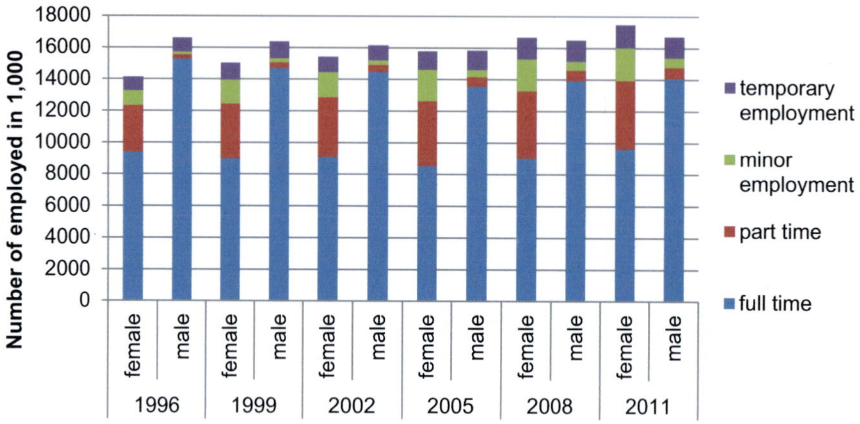

Source: Mikrozensus; own illustration.

Figure 6: Types of employment

In almost all kinds of atypical employment, women dominate. In contrast to normally employed individuals, the atypically employed face greater social risks and mainly work under precarious conditions. This also impacts the pension entitlements in a negative way. In general, the wages and therefore the contributions as well as private savings are generally lower and there are more periods of unemployment during the career. Moreover, transitions into full-time employment are rare.[48]

Another trend in the labor market is the increasing number of self-employed, who are not obligated to pay contributions to the public pension insurance. About 11% of all employed were self-employed in 2010.[49] The increase in the number of solo self-employed, i.e., self-employed without other employees, is the main cause of the trend. In analyzing this subgroup some specific characteristics can be identified: solo self-employment contains more and more jobs that were primarily done in dependent employment (e.g. nursing or cleaning): the period of self-employment is rather short and in most situations the transition into dependent employment or unemployment,

[47] Forms of atypical employment are: partial employment, minor employment, temporary employment and subcontracted work.

[48] See Keller and Seifert (2011), Wingerter (2009) and Steiner and Geyer (2010).

[49] See KFW (2012).

the income level, as well as level of wealth is low for many solo self-employed, often they are older and also women tend to become solo self-employed.[50] Since there is no regulation for a compulsory retirement provision for the self-employed, most of them do not save enough or even at all for their retirement. The latest pension reform package for 2013 provides regulations for a compulsory pension insurance for self-employed in order to avoid old-age poverty. The proposal includes several choices for a pension system. The idea of integrating all self-employed into the public pension system to expand the number of contributors did not get a wide acceptance. In particular, Gasche and Rausch (2012) evaluated such a compulsory insurance and concluded that potential gains for the pension insurance can be only expected in the short-run. Assuming a higher average life expectancy of the self-employed, the integration might even worsen the financial sustainability of the public pension system in the long run.

The German pension system is strongly linked to the employment history. Full-time employment without any interruptions is necessary to obtain an adequate pension at the end of the career. While this was the case for the majority of men in the past, nowadays more and more individuals do have discontinuous and/or precarious employment biographies.[51] Further, the expanding low wage sector makes it more difficult to obtain a sufficient level of pension entitlement.[52] Despite the efforts to devolve some responsibility of old-age provision on individuals, the public pension is still the major source of income for the elderly. As it is presented in the old-age provision report of the federal government 64%, of gross income of individuals aged 65+ comes from the public pension. Private pensions account for 9%. Occupational pensions are even more negligible with 8%.[53]

Occupational pensions, as the second tier of old-age provision, do not play a significant role in Germany yet, but the importance is rising. In 2007, about 50% of all employees had some occupational pension entitlements.[54] A slight increase can be observed, e.g.

[50] See Koch et al. (2011).

[51] See Trischler and Kistler (2010).

[52] See Bosch (2012).

[53] See Bundesregierung (2012a).

[54] See Bundesregierung (2008), p. 126.

in 2011, 56% of all employees had some occupational pension entitlements. Among these employees, more highly educated persons as well as persons with a higher income acquire disproportionately often occupational pension entitlements.[55]

As mentioned before, private pensions, mainly in form of Riester pensions, are criticized for poor product design and low rates of return. To close the pension gap a savings rate of 4% of gross earnings into a Riester contract is necessary. Moreover, a long period of saving between 25 and 30 years is essential, as Börsch-Supan and Gasche (2010) have shown. In addition, even though the participation rate has risen over the last years, still, less than 50% of all eligible persons have a contract. Coppola and Gasche (2011) provide evidence for the fact that knowledge about the eligibility for subsidies for the Riester pension is mostly lacking for lower income households. Also the unemployed and individuals receiving a basic protection for the needy ("Grundsicherung") are less likely to hold a Riester pension.[56] However, these groups are supposed to be the target group.

According to a recent study (BMAS 2012) conducted in 2011 by the government, the co-occurrence of occupational entitlements and a Riester pension is rather rare. As can be seen from Table 3, 20% of employees have entitlements from both occupational and Riester pensions. Indeed, the majority of employees (36%) does not hold a Riester pension plan but does participate in an occupational pension plan. 29% of all employees neither have an occupational pension nor a Riester pension. The fact that an occupational pension plan is not offered by the company or employer, is the major reason, as stated by 48% of the respondents, for the lack of participation. Concerning the non-existent Riester pension the most named reason was the participation in other pension plans. Not being able to afford the contributions was a reason for 23% of employees in case of a Riester pension, and 18% in case of an occupational pension. In both cases 11% of all employees do not inform themselves about the topic at all, and may therefore underestimate the importance of additional old-age provisions.

---

[55] See BMAS (2012).

[56] See Promberger et al. (2012).

		Occupational pension entitlements	
		Yes	*No*
Riester pension entitlements	*Yes*	20%	15%
	No	36%	29%

Table 3: Co-occurrence of pension entitlements of employees liable to social security contributions aged between 25 and 65

Overall, the focus on public pensions as the major source of old-age provisions indicates that any reforms, especially those that reduce pensions, affect old-age poverty quite directly. The intention of most pension reforms was to decrease the generosity. The downward development of the net pension level before tax[57] reflects this. In 1985 it was over 57.4%, whereas in 2012 it is 49.6%.[58] Forecasts of the federal government state a net pension level before tax of 43% in 2030.[59]

The poverty rate of persons aged 65+ was 15.3% in 2011 and is below the average rate for the whole society, which was 19.9%.[60] The German social security provides a means-tested[61] basic protection for persons who have an income below the subsistence level. It benefits individuals aged 65 and older or adults who are permanently fully incapable of work. The number of retirees who are eligible for this basic protection has increased in recent years and reached 435,210 in 2012. Compared to the whole society the proportion is less than 3%, which is quite low, but the tendency is rising. It will become more and more difficult to obtain a pension amount above the subsistence level. Figure 7 illustrates the increasing number of years of contribution in dependency of the earnings level. In 2010, the net pension level before tax was 51.6%. To obtain a pension in the amount of the subsistence level, which was 670€ in 2010, an average earner has

---

[57] The net pension level before tax is the ratio between the net standard pension, i.e. a pension of an insurant who paid 45 years of contribution on the basis of the average earnings, and the average income of the same year.

[58] See Deutsche Rentenversicherung Bund (2011).

[59] See Bundesregierung (2012b).

[60] Data from Federal Statistical Office.

[61] An entitlement is only given after taking into account other forms of income including income of all household members.

to fulfill 27.1 years of contribution. An employee earning 70% of the average wage needs 38.7 years. Under the assumption of declining pension levels in the future, the number of contribution years will increase. According to a pension level of 46.2% predicted by the federal government for 2025, an average earner has to contribute for an additional 3 years, whereas a person earning 70% of the average wage needs 43.2 years of contributions to reach a pension amount above the subsistence level. Such a number of years is unlikely to be achieved, due to later entry into the labor force and several periods of unemployment in general. Finally, the legitimation of paying contributions for years in order to receive a pension that equals only the subsistence level can be questioned.

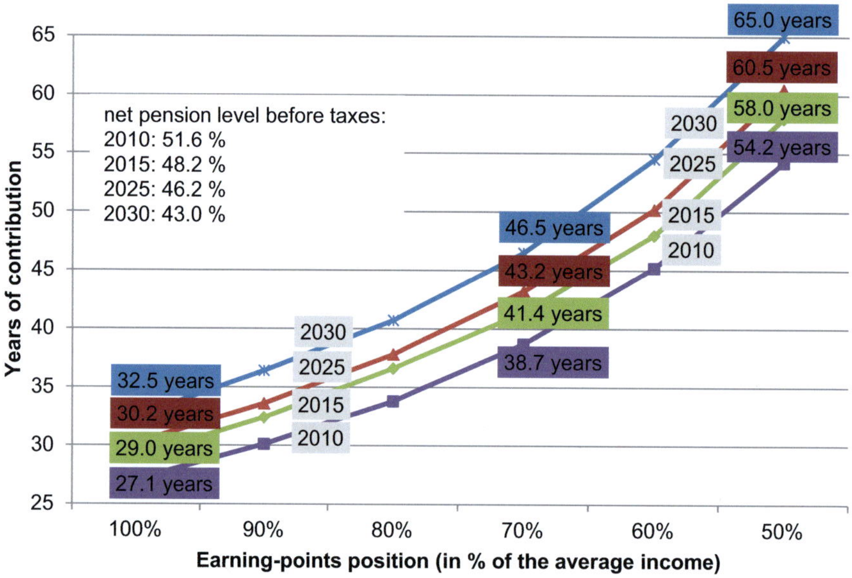

Assumptions:
Basic security at old-age (SGB XII): Requirements of a single person (standard benefit and costs of housing) in the year 2010: 670€; pension: net pension before taxes; pension level 2010, 2015, 2025 according to the report of annuity insurance 2011, 2030: minimum level of the level protection clause

Source: Sozialpolitik aktuell – Figure VIII.54; own translation.

Figure 7: Overlapping of basic security and pensions by decreasing pension level

Working after retirement is conceivable for almost one in every two employees above 55. In fact, only every tenth retiree has employment. Considering data from the German

Socio-Economic Panel Study (SEOP), about 5.8% of retirees are working regularly, mainly in mini-jobs or independent activities.[62]

Data from the FSO shows a continuous decline in the employment rate from the age of 55 onwards (see Figure 8), whereas, the total share of employed elderly has risen over the past years. Taking a look at Figure 9, it is striking that self-employment occupies a higher proportion the older the employed are.

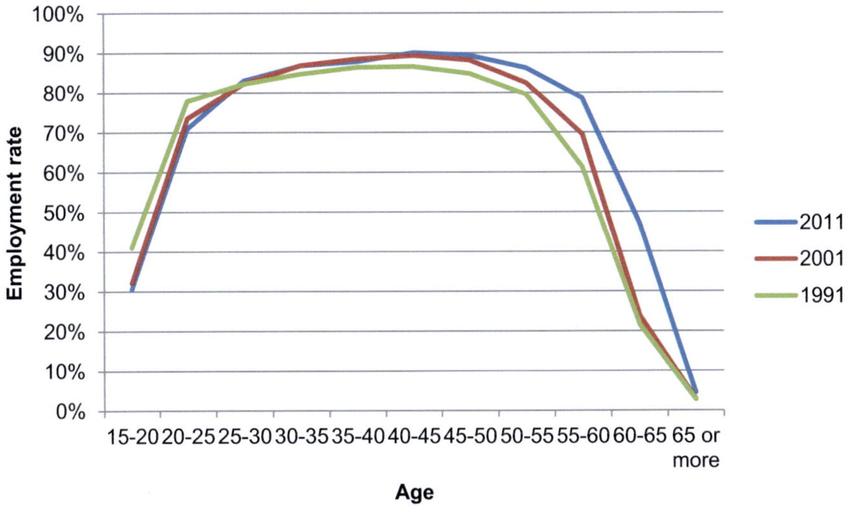

Source: German Federal Statistical Office; own illustration.

Figure 8: Employment rate by age groups

[62] See IWD (2010).

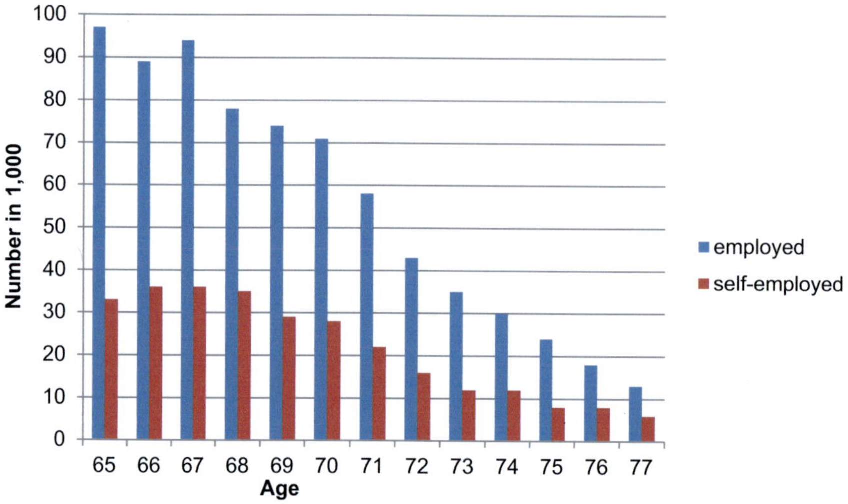

Source: German Federal Statistical Office; own illustration.

Figure 9: Number of employed and self-employed persons in Germany in 2011

In conclusion, modern employment biographies are less stable, shorter and therefore less likely to provide a sufficient pension entitlement. Insurants still trust the promise of secure public pensions and still have their own grandparents in mind, who receive a quite satisfactory pension. Reducing the generosity of the pension system was a reasonable way for the government to counter future demographic challenges. Next, in order to stem old-age poverty, political attempts should be focused on labor activities of the elderly to cope with the changes in modern careers.

3 Adapting the retirement system

After having discussed the various challenges of an aging society in Chapter 2, this chapter focusses on the potentials that derive from it. To be able to benefit from an extended lifespan, the additional years have to be spent in mental and physical fitness. Thus, a separate examination of health expectancy is necessary. A worldwide glance at other pension systems follows in order to outline best practices as well as innovative research. Lastly, recent labor market developments are analyzed as a baseline for potential interventions.

3.1 Life vs. health expectancy

The old-age dependency ratio (OADR) reflects the proportion of the working age population[63] in comparison to the elderly, i.e. the population aged 65 and up. In 2010 Germany had the highest ratio at 31.3, among the EU countries. Consistent with the increasing life expectancy, also this ratio rises over time and is often used to state the burden of the elderly shouldered by the younger population. A more optimistic ratio is the prospective old-age dependency ratio (POADR) that contrasts individuals with a further life expectancy of more than 15 years with individuals with having a further life expectancy of less than 15 years. This ratio is supposed to increase more slowly over time, as in Figure 10. The proportion of the population 20+ in need of help in contrast to the proportion of the population 20+ able to give help is reflected by the adult disability dependency ratio (ADDR). The ADDR will rise only slightly in the future and is supposed to have a value of 0.13 in 2028.[64]

---

[63] I. e. the population between 15 and 65 years.

[64] See BMFSJ (2012).

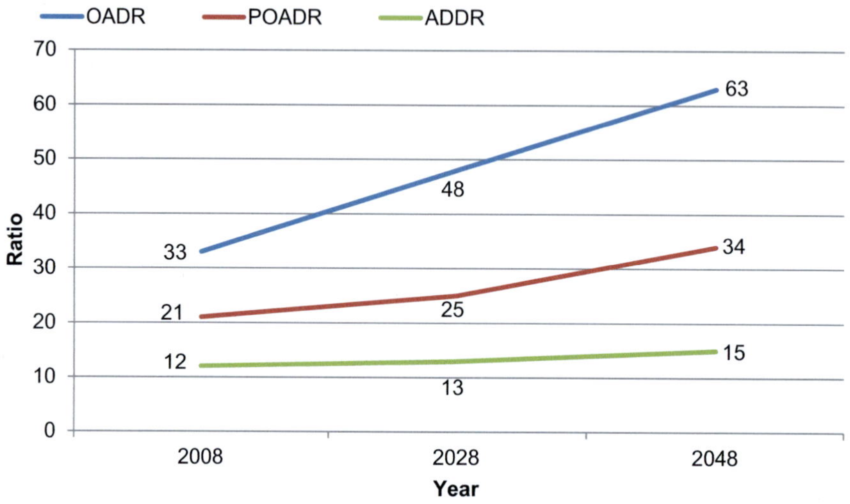

Source: Scherbov and Sanderson (2010), p. 2; own illustration based on BMFSJ (2012), p. 12.

Figure 10: The age dependency ratio and alternative ratios

Regarding the future development of the health status of the elderly, two opposite theories exist in the literature. On the one hand, the *Expansion of Morbidity* theory by Gruenberg (1977) indicates that the successful postponing of the death of ill individuals often just prolongs the suffering. Thus, the gain in life expectancy comes with a longer period of chronic diseases and need of care. In contrast, Fries (1980) states the *Compression of Morbidity* theory, which indicates a postponement of diseases and need of care during the life time. In between, Manton (1982) argues for an equal increase of both periods, which is named the *Dynamic Equilibrium* theory. Therefore, the gain in life expectancy is divided more or less equally into healthy and unhealthy years. In a review by Robine and Michel (2004), the authors draw a temporary conclusion that all three situations coexist today. A forecast about the domination of one specific theory needs further research in the field of population aging.

The World Health Organization (WHO) defines health as "a state of complete physical, mental and social well-being and not merely the absence of disease or infirmity" (WHO (1946), p. 1). After more than sixty years of medical and sociological progress this definition has not changed but still prevails. Difficulties arising from measuring health properly are the major problem in defining a general standard of the valuation of health. Either diagnoses of disease symptoms or of the ability to perform activities of daily living (ADL)[65] as well as the ability to perform instrumental activities of daily living (IADL)[66] can be used to assess the individual's health status. In most studies a self-assessment of the respondents takes place. Although biased by the personality as well as the social background of the individual[67], self-reported health status is an important indicator of the individual's overall well-being.[68]

For many research questions about population aging, health expectancy, instead of life expectancy, is the decisive factor and therefore needs to be measured accurately. This is especially true for pension systems, since the health status determines the retirement age. Murray et al. (2000) divides measures of population health into two groups: health expectancies and health gaps. The first is determined quite obviously by subtracting the number of years with health impairment from the total number of expected living years deriving the corresponding parameters *health-adjusted life expectancy* (HALE) or *disability-free life expectancy* (DFLE). The second is the difference between the actual health status of a population and a defined target value. Corresponding parameters for health gaps are *quality adjusted life years* (QALYs) and *disability adjusted life years* (DALYs). A general distinction is drawn between dichotomous health states weights (e.g. used in DFLE) and a set of health states weights differing with the level of disability (e.g. used in HALE).[69]

Measuring health expectancy requires information about mortality and morbidity. The mortality component is represented by age-specific death rates. This information is provided by official statistics of developed states and has a high quality. In contrast, information for the morbidity component is usually drawn from surveys based on self-assessment of the individuals or medical diagnoses. Overall trends are difficult to analyze because of heterogeneous designs, nonresponses and sample selections bias.

---

[65] The ADL index was established by Katz et al. (1963) and measures over-all performance in bathing, dressing, going to the toilet, mobility, continence, and feeding.

[66] Lawton and Brody (1969) extended the fundamental functions of the ADL index by functions required for independent living in a community like shopping, using technology and handling finances.

[67] See Sadana et al. (2002).

[68] See e.g. Kahneman and Krueger (2006) or Mueller and Heinzel-Gutenbrunner (2001).

[69] See Mathers (2002).

Nevertheless, both components are combined into a single one, representing healthy life expectancy, using life table methodology. The most common method to measure health expectancy was introduced by Sullivan (1971). In this method the number of survivors in a population is reduced by the number of survivors who are unhealthy (however this might be defined). In doing so, the number of healthy survivors is determined and a new life table for a certain period is constructed. Only age-specific data of mortality and morbidity is necessary, making this method very straight-forward. Substituting prevalence with incidence, double decrement life tables are able to quantify short-term changes in incidence better than the Sullivan method.[70] Further, accounting for the fact that disabilities as well as diseases could be reversible, multi-state life tables provide adequate rates regarding the interactions between morbidity and mortality. Rogers et al. (1989) were the first, who used such a calculation method. The necessity of age-specific incidences of transitions between healthy and unhealthy states limits the application of this method, since such data is only seldom available. Thus, for the reason of minimal complexity by providing relatively similar results[71], the Sullivan method is predominantly used.

Statistical data for Germany about healthy life years is provided by the statistical office of the EU Eurostat. The annual European Statistics on Income and Living Conditions (EU-SILC)[72] survey includes a question about the individual's limitations in activities caused by health problems.[73] By means of the responses, the prevalence of disability and the indicator healthy life years are calculated using the Sullivan method. Figure 11 includes the average life expectancy and healthy life years at age 65 for females and males in Germany between 2005 and 2011. While there is a clear gap in life expectancy between females and males, the difference in gender for healthy life years is only minor.[74] On average a women aged 65 is supposed to have seven healthy life years, which is about 34% of their remaining life expectancy. Males aged 65 are supposed to still have 6.9

[70] See Katz et al. (1983).

[71] See Mathers and Robine (1997).

[72] See Atkinson and Marlier (2010).

[73] The EU-SILC does not include the institutionalized population and therefore, underestimates the prevalence of morbidity.

[74] Similar results for the US population are also found by Case and Paxon (2005).

healthy life years on average, which is about 40% of their remaining life expectancy. Data was not collected prior to 2005. Thus, a trend regarding healthy life years cannot be identified validly. Lafortune and Balestat (2007) reveal in a projection for the OECD positive trends of disability as well as negative ones depending on the country. Likewise, the analysis of Kroll et al. (2005), who compared several health measures in various countries, does not indicate a clear trend as to whether the healthy life years will increase or decrease in the future. Meanwhile, they identify, examining several studies, a higher health expectancy for individuals with a higher education, higher occupational status and higher income.[75] This holds independently from gender for the US, for Germany and other European states.

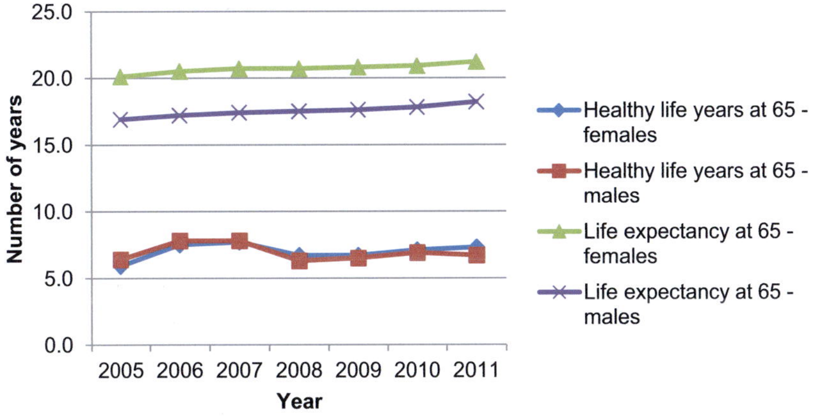

Source: Eurostat for death and population data, Eurostat SILC for activity limitation; own illustration.

Figure 11: Average life expectancy and healthy life years at age 65 in Germany between 2005 and 2011

As can be seen in analyzing some characteristics of the elderly, some relevant aspects influencing the health status threaten the expansion of morbidity. Overweight is significantly more prevalent with increasing age, the men dominating at all ages. This factor comes with a higher risk for many diseases. The highest proportion of overweight

[75] The positive effect of higher education, higher income and higher occupational status on life expectancy is also verifiable by comparing retirees and civil service pensioners. The latter normally belong to the group of more highly educated and situated employees. But even within both groups the differences hold (See Himmelreicher et al. (2008)).

persons is in the age group of 70 to 74. In this group, in 2009, almost three quarters of all men are overweight and almost two thirds of all women.[76]

Regarding hospital cases, the major group of inpatients (43% in 2009) is 65 or older. Moreover, the period of hospitalization is on average longer for women than for men, but in total has shortened over the past years.[77]

Nursing is analyzed in the nursing statistics since 1999 in Germany. Since then, only a small increase of 0.4% in the number of cases could be observed. In 2009 about 2.3 Mio persons were classified as in need of care. The risk of requiring nursing increases strongly with age, as shown in Table 4. More than one in two persons over 90 is in need of care, women three times as often as men.[78]

Age	In total	Men	Women
Under 15	0.6	0.6	0.6
15 – 59	0.5	0.5	0.5
60 – 64	1.7	1.7	1.6
65 – 69	2.7	2.8	2.5
70 – 74	4.7	4.7	4.8
75 – 79	9.9	8.8	10.7
80 – 85	19.9	15.7	22.3
85 – 89	38	28.3	41.6
90 and older	59.1	36.8	66.7
In total	2.9	1.9	3.8

Table 4: Share of persons in need of care within the German population in 2009 in per cent

[76] See Statistisches Bundesamt (2011), p. 74.

[77] See Statistisches Bundesamt (2011), p. 76.

[78] See Statistisches Bundesamt (2011), p. 82.

The number of severely disabled persons also increases with age. Over half of them have an age of 65 or higher. Within the group of 80+ every third person (31%) has a severely disabled person's pass.[79]

Anyhow, as the total number of the elderly increases, many of the stated aspects are also influenced. A necessary decrease in individual health status does not follow. Even though no clear trend can be identified by research, nothing contradicts so far a general increase in healthy life expectancy in the future.

3.2 The global retirement landscape

The Melbourne Mercer Global Pension Index[80] ranks annually 18 countries and covers over half of the world's population. Taking into account public funded as well as private components of the pension system, as well as savings and personal assets, the index controls for more than 40 indicators. In doing so, three major fields are evaluated: adequacy, sustainability and integrity. The final scores range from 0 to 100 resulting in grades of A to E. In 2012 Denmark was on top of the ranking and the first country ever classified as A with an overall index value of 82.9. Germany was given a score of 55.3 with a corresponding rank of 15th. Further, the Melbourne Mercer Global Pension index provides country-specific suggestions for improvement. The recommendations for Germany are:

- to enforce the payment of pension benefits as an income stream,
- to communicate more clearly the pension arrangements to the members,
- to raise the participation rate of the elderly in the labor market,
- to increase the minimum pension.

In the course of the analysis, this thesis especially contributes to the last two of them.

In 2011 the Allianz Global Investors published a Pension Sustainability Index[81] including 44 countries. Compared to the Melbourne Mercer Global Pension Index mentioned

[79] See Statistisches Bundesamt (2011), p. 84.

[80] Refer to Melbourne Centre for Financial Studies and Mercer (2012) for full details.

[81] Refer to Allianz Global Investors (2011a) for full details.

before, the rating of pension systems differs only slightly. Still, Denmark belongs to the top 3, whereas Germany is ranked the midfield (No. 19). In general, the survey highlights the fundamental reforms of many western European countries since 1995, delivering them to some extent from the *"Bismarck's pension trap"*[82]. The governments have abandoned the tradition of public pensions being the main income source of the elderly. Instead, the states have implemented a multi-tiered structure of retirement income fostering funded pension plans. This changes the structure of private households' assets, as shown in Figure 12. The share of pension plans and insurance products increased in Western Europe between 1996 and 2010. Japan, which is ranked at the bottom of the index, shows the lowest amount. Since occupational and private pension plans are more common in the US, corresponding changes over time are minor.

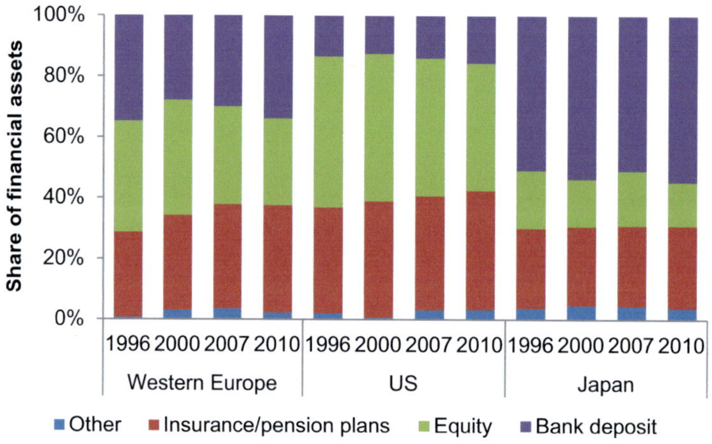

Source: own illustration modified from Allianz Global Investors (2011b), p. 9.

Figure 12: Financial assets' structure

Moreover, the Global Pension Atlas 2011 was published by Allianz Global Investors in the same year and has the intention of providing a cogent and informative map of the global pension landscape including major trends since the multitude of reforms in the 1990s. The study detects a shift in funded pensions of the occupational pillar from defined benefit to defined contribution plans. In this way, the companies pass the risk on to the workers. In addition to that, private pension plans are asking too much of

[82] This phrase indicates the collapse of the PAYGO system due to the demographic changes (see Zimmerer (2012), p. 6).

many individuals, since they hesitate to participate in a private pension plan at all. Further, individuals have problem identifying the amount as well as the adequate form of investment. The study identifies a positive correlation between the participation rate of private pension plans and the generosity of the public system.[83]

Behavioral economics takes emotional, cognitive and social aspects of the individual's economic decision into account. Hence, through this, a more realistic approach is enabled and can be used for highly sensitive decisions like retirement plans. Inertia, i.e. the lack of action, plays an essential role in retirement provision. In line with this, Bernartzi and Thaler (2004) propose the SMarT (Save More Tomorrow) program that is a prescriptive saving program. With the purpose of overcoming self-control and bounded rationality problems, this program causes participants to save ex ante a portion of their coming salary increases for retirement. After implementing the program in three different companies, they demonstrate a high participation rate, a low exit rate and an increase in the average savings rates of the participants. Thus, they successfully take advantage of inertia and procrastination by automatic enrollment and pushing off the commitment to save into the future.

So far, mandatory occupational or private pension schemes have been introduced in only few countries but the tendency towards it is present. Thus, worldwide pension assets are growing. Countries with a tradition of funded pillars like the US, the United Kingdom, Switzerland and the Netherlands have high asset volumes compared to GDP, whereas asset volumes of countries in central and eastern Europe are much lower, since they started to build up funded assets just a couple of years ago (see Figure 13).

[83] See Allianz Global Investors (2011c).

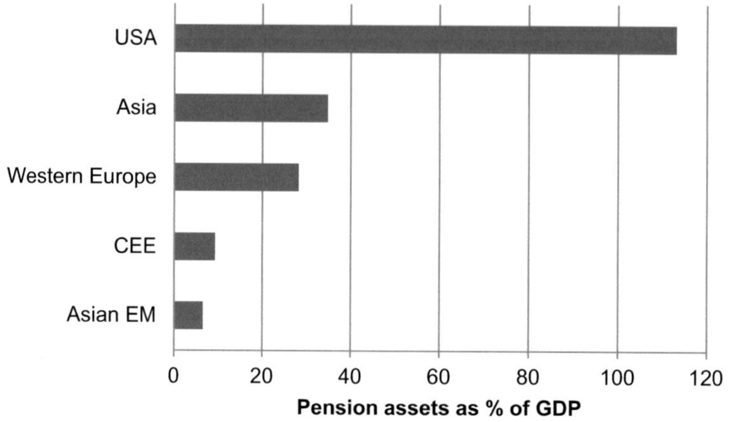

Source: own illustration modified from Allianz Global Investors (2011c), p. 13.

Figure 13: Worldwide pension assets

The size of funded pensions belonging to the occupational and private pillar correlates negatively with the generosity of the public pension system. In line with this, the US, the United Kingdom, Switzerland and the Netherlands have strong funded pensions on the one hand and low replacement rates deriving from the public pension scheme on the other. Due to the ongoing reduction of the state's responsibility to provide sufficient pensions in Central and Eastern Europe as well as in Asia, pension assets will grow further at higher rates in these countries. Though a balance of the three pillars is aspired by the countries, pension systems still are quite different. Figure 14 illustrates the heterogeneity of the global pension systems with regard to the development of funded pension schemes. In particular, the transition progress towards a defined contribution system as well as the overall proportion of funded pension assets as percentage of GDP are mapped. At the bottom there is Greece, colored yellow, as a country with very low funded pension assets and no obvious intention to make changes concerning this matter.

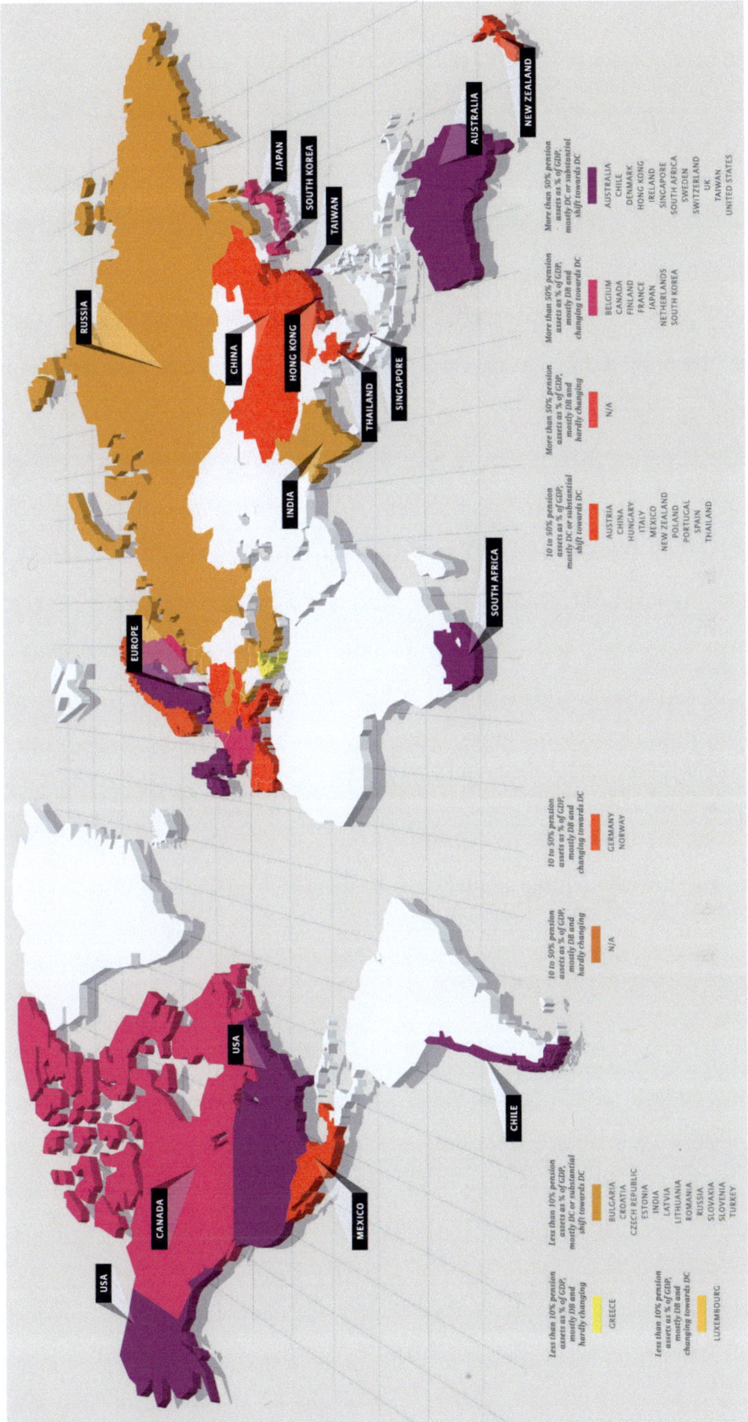

Source: Allianz Global Investors (2011c), p. 19.

Figure 14: The global pension atlas

Most east European countries, including Germany, Russia and India are arranged in the mid field, colored dark yellow and red. At the top of the ranking, colored pink and violet, are western European and Scandinavian countries, the US, Australia, Chile, South Africa and some Asian countries.[84]

Holzmann (2012), a Senior Advisor to the World Bank, evaluates systematically global pension systems. In his study the prevalence of funded defined contribution schemes is observable and confirms the global transition back from unfunded defined benefit schemes mentioned in the previous paragraphs. The study further stresses the movement in objectives, reforms and conditions of pension systems, like focusing on basic income provision, ensuring solvency and strengthening the participation of the elderly in the labor market. These targets are mainly in line with the agenda of the White Paper by the European Commission (2012b). In general, the public pension represents the first pillar. Stating Chile's reforms as a benchmark, a zero pillar, providing basic income to keep the elderly from poverty, is somehow implemented in the majority of countries worldwide. Only a few countries have introduced an additional covering in form of a second pillar. In Europe only Poland did so. Rather, effort is put into fostering the third pillar by spreading information and lowering costs of enrollment, guaranteeing a minimum limit of performance[85] or providing tax benefits for private pensions. E.g. the Mbao program in Kenya enables making deposits into private pension savings accounts via mobile phones.[86] Especially, employees of the growing informal sector are covered through such a savings form.

The global trend towards a wider base of funded pension assets is ongoing. Thus, worldwide pension assets are expected to grow. The financial crises dampened the optimism about the funded pensions as a sustainable and secure old-age income. A diverse old-age provision is needed to ensure living standards in retirement. In order to make the right savings decisions the individual's financial literacy is essential. In

[84] See Allianz Global Investors (2011c).

[85] Joebges et al. (2012) contrast rates of return of the public pension scheme and the Riester Rente, i.e. the private pension scheme in Germany. By comparing different studies and simulations the rates of return of the private schemes are in general lower, achieving even only half the amount of the public pension scheme.

[86] See ISSA (2011).

addition, the government should make use of behavioral finance approaches to support welfare.

3.3 Labor market developments

In spite the increasing total number of the elderly due to the demographic change, the employment rate of the elderly rose above average between 2000 and 2010. Comparing the rates of employed persons aged between 15 and 65 (+5.6%), Figure 15 indicates an ongoing increase in the employment rate in correlation with age groups. Thus, the increase is the highest for the age group between 60 and 65 with +20.9%, which is even more than a doubling of the value.[87]

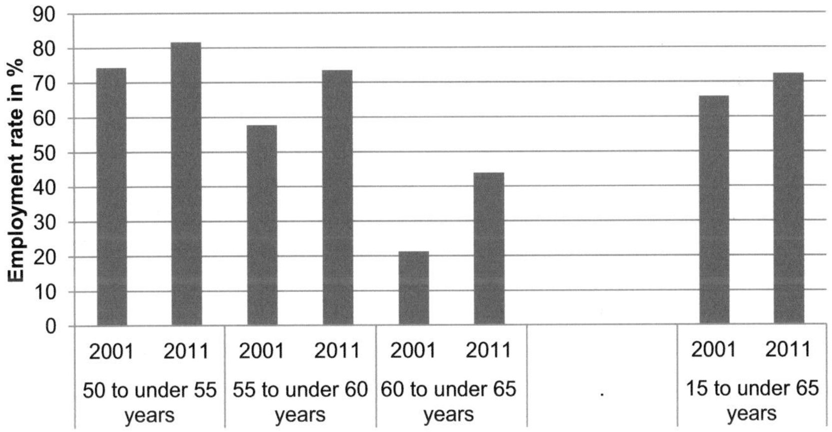

Source: Mikrozensus; own illustration.

Figure 15: Employment rates 2001 and 2011

Regarding the jobs of the elderly, self-employment, family workers and civil servants dominate. Since 2000, all these groups achieved an increase in the total number, the group of white-collar employees increasing the most. Moreover, the proportion of part-time employment rises with age and reaches the highest value of 29% within the group of employed persons aged between 60 and 65.[88]

[87] See Bundesagentur für Arbeit (2012).
[88] See Bundesagentur für Arbeit (2012).

The development of the unemployment rate of the elderly shows different directions. Between 2007 and 2011 a decrease in the unemployment rate for the age groups 50 – 55 and 55 – 60 can be noticed, whereas the unemployment rate of the age group 60 – 65 quadrupled. This discrepancy is shown in Figure 16. Since the chances for reentry into the labor market are lower the older the person is, the period of unemployment rises with age. In line with this, a higher proportions of unemployed persons aged 50+ are permanently unemployed, i.e. for more than 12 months, which is 45%, comparing to the average of all age groups at a third.[89]

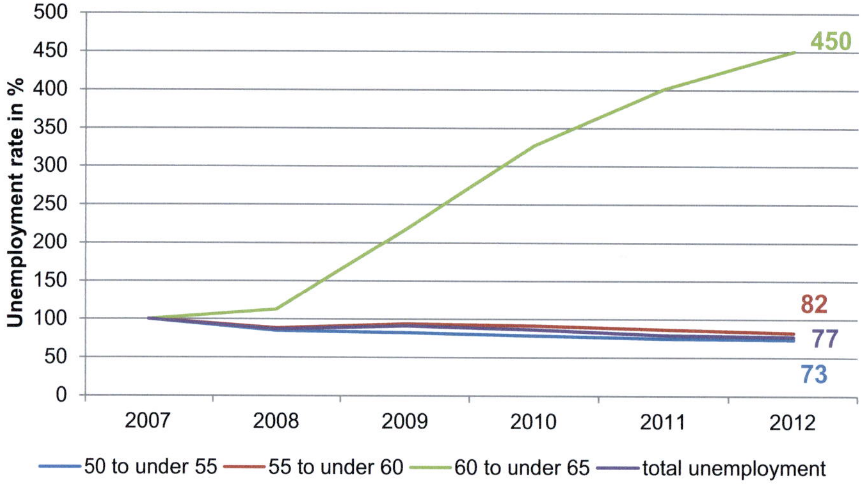

Notes: average annual values in percent (2007 = 100%).

Source: Federal Employment Agency; own illustration.

Figure 16: Unemployment rates 2007 – 2012

Reasons behind a change in the labor force of a certain age group can be either a change in the size of the age group or changes in the labor force participation rate. The first derives from changes within the structure of a population, like an increase or a decrease in the size of a certain age group. In this case, the reason would be demographic developments. The other option is that the behavior of people who are available for the labor market changes within a certain age group. This affects the labor force participation rate of this age group. Both effects hold true for Germany in regard

[89] See Bundesagentur für Arbeit (2012).

to the age group 65+. However, the rise in the positive attitude towards employment is responsible for about 80% of the total increase in the labor force.[90]

Regarding employment above the age of 65, the characteristics are even more distinctive. One out of two employees was self-employed or a family worker. Further, over two third (69%) worked part-time.[91] The jobs that are performed beyond the age of 65 are various. On the one hand, many of the elderly work as executives or in academic positions. On the other hand, many have simple jobs in the service industry or in farming.[92]

Financial motives do not seem to play the leading role according to a recent study. Here, besides the income earned during retirement, most of the employees over 65 achieve a household income above the poverty level. In fact, on average, employed retirees are more generally satisfied than unemployed retirees. The greater satisfaction refers to the living, the wealth and the health status.[93]

A study from the Federal Institute for Population Research (BiB) in 2008 questioned 1,500 employees aged between 55 and 64 about ongoing employment at retirement age. Only a minority shows a willingness to do so, since they strongly prefer to spent time with the family and enjoy their retirement. The major motivation to continue employment is to stay fit. According to the participants, the prior role of the government is to enable flexibility and promote good health. Further, the study shows only small differences between public and private employees. Thus, employment at higher ages is conceivable for the respondents, but comes along with shortened working times.[94] Similar findings derive from a Europe-wide study conducted in 2011 on behalf of the European Commission. Almost half of the respondents want to work after reaching retirement age. Again, part time and reduced working hours are strongly preferred. Consequently, poor possibilities to exit the labor force gradually, unfavorable

[90] See Brenke (2013).

[91] See Statistisches Bundesamt (2011), p. 47.

[92] See Brenke (2013).

[93] See Brenke (2013).

[94] Over 70% of the participants prefer working between 10 and 24 hours per week (see Büsch et al. (2010)).

attitudes of the employers towards the elderly as well as a lack of qualification are mentioned as major reasons for quitting the job from the age of 55 onwards.[95]

For a long-lasting and successful integration into the labor market, the elderly have to be able to work, i.e., have to fulfill criteria concerning health, competence and motivation. But they also have to be employable. That means that the labor market has to be open to the elderly and companies have to provide adequate working conditions.[96] Bellmann et al. stated in 2007 that companies failed to adapt themselves to the demographic change. There is a lack of continuing education, workplace health promotion as well as work organization, all of which would have a positive effect on the employment of the elderly.

In order to keep the elderly in employment an interaction at different levels is needed. Companies, labor unions, the government and employees themselves have to cooperate and foster adequate activities. As the labor unions are limited by the legal framework in their transition process, the government should allow for more flexibility through corresponding reform acts.[97] Companies also still have not exhausted the potential for implementing specific measures for the elderly, so called *"age management measures"*[98]. According to the IAB Establishment Panel[99] of 2008 only 17% of companies with employees above 50 years of age provide such measures at all. Most of them are companies with more than 250 employees and belong to the public sector or the credit and insurance industry. Although the measures have to be adapted to the characteristics of the company and the personnel structure, a distinction between three main fields of action is reasonable:

---

[95] See European Commission (2012c).

[96] See the results of the study by Ilmarinen (2006).

[97] See Fehmel (2011).

[98] See Naegele and Walker (2006).

[99] The IAB Establishment Panel is an annual and nationwide employer survey of employment parameters at almost 16,000 establishments covering all branches of the economy.

- *Qualification*: the lifelong learning of all employees is necessary to keep the individual's innovativeness and productivity.
- *Health promotion*: offering a range of health services and an ergonomic workplace influence the cognitive and physical ability of the employees in a positive way and therefore, is beneficial for both, the employer and the employee.
- *Labor organization*: arrangements in regard to working times, age-based employment and careers in a forward-looking manner allow for long-time employment.[100]

The higher the number of age management measures offered by the company, the better the self-evaluation of the working ability of the elderly. This is one of the results of a study conducted in 2010. About 80% of elderly employees are convinced that they would be able to perform well in their job until the legal retirement age if the companies offer seven or more age management measures. If no measures are offered to the respondents, only one of two says so. Further, the number of measures correlates positively with job satisfaction.[101] Some recommendations for qualification measures are given by Leve and Zimmer (2011). To meet the highest level of efficiency, measures should be offered during the whole employment history of an individual.

In recent years, lifelong learning has become more and more an essential element of the human resource policy and follows an ongoing positive trend. Since 1979 the participation rate in continuing education has been quantified and reached the highest value in 2012 with 49%. Especially on-the-job training as well as not job-related continuing education gained remarkable importance. Employers seem to notice the effectiveness of qualified employees and invest in their education by meeting the costs to an increasing extent and allowing for further education during working hours. Although the participation rate of the elderly (60–64 years old) is lower than the participation rate of younger employees (18–59 years old), namely, 32% compared to about 50%, the rate is still relatively high.[102] However, older as well as lower qualified

---

[100] See BMAS (2010), p. 73.

[101] See Wirtschaftsfaktor Alter (2010).

[102] See BMBF (2013).

persons in general have a lower participation rate than younger and higher qualified persons.[103] Greater effort has to be made by the companies in closing this gap in order to promote the productivity of the elderly and support further education of lower qualified employees.

In supporting a work-life balance, German companies already perform quite well. According to a recent study of the Cologne Institute for Economic Research for the Ministry of Family Affairs, Senior Citizens, Women and Youth, about 99% of all companies support a better compatibility of work and family.[104] About 80% of the 1,556 companies questioned see the work-life balance as an essential part of in their strategy. Three out of four companies assume this importance will even increase in the next five years. The most common measure is an individual working time arrangement. By offering this, the company allows for the care of children or parents in need of care. About one quarter of all companies release their employees from work in case a family member is in need of care. Almost the same share also uses the option of a temporary work reduction. In doing so, the employee reduces his or her working hours, while the salary, though reduced, is not reduced by the equivalent amount. After the period of care, the employee works again at regular working hours. The salary remains reduced until his or her time account is balanced. Such concession by of the employers is essential in promoting employability. Both childcare and the care of older family members require flexible working hours on an individual level. This keeps the employees on their jobs and does not lead to interruptions of employment, which directly affects pension claims in a negative way.

Apart from keeping employees, recruiting is also a key part of human resource management. In contrast to the increasing share of employed elderly, the number of elderly being recruited has not increased during the last number of years. Especially lower qualified individuals are affected by this, since higher qualified individuals usually have more stable jobs and face a lower risk of job loss. Thus, there is still selectivity in regard to age in recruiting new staff members, to the disadvantage of the elderly.[105]

---

[103] See Leber et. al (2013).
[104] See BMFSJ (2013).
[105] See Brussig (2011a) and Dietz and Walwei (2011).

Wübbeke (2012) studies the reasons why long-term unemployed individuals exit the labor force and shows that low or no propensity to work is not a relevant motive, but rather bad recruiting prospects. Nevertheless, the elderly still offer a high potential. While cardiopulmonary capacity and muscular strength decline with age, which can lead to long-term health impairments and chronic diseases, social capital rises with age. Ideally, physical drawbacks are compensated by gains in expertise, routine and professional networks.[106] The work ability index, which is broadly used in research and has been tested by several international studies, can be used for controlling purposes.[107] Assessing work ability helps to identify adequate measures to avoid a decline. The ELMA study confirms potential for physical and cognitive improvement even at higher ages where there are qualification and trainings.[108] A better education, furthermore, enhances the chances for ongoing employment after the retirement age, since a positive correlation has been detected.[109]

At the beginning of the coming decade more than a quarter of the population of working age will be older than 55.[110] Krumm et al. (2012) have shown in a study that job satisfaction increases with age. The reason for this is the better fit of expectations about the job to the reality and therefore less disappointment of the elderly. In order to keep the elderly motivated and satisfied the companies have to enhance the potentials of the elderly, e.g., knowledge transfer to the younger generation. This can be done by mentoring or age-mixed working teams. Companies have to take the elderly more strongly into account, leading to a further increase of the employment rate of the elderly and a better adaption to the demographic change. There are already some public programs promoting employment of the elderly and rewarding the companies who do. On the other hand several companies have acted as pioneers and invented autonomously specific internal programs for the elderly.

[106] See Ilmarinen (2012).

[107] See Ilmarinen (2007) and Ilmarinen (2009).

[108] See Kruse et al. (2010).

[109] See Bäcker et. al (2009), Brussig (2011b) and Micheel and Panova (2013).

[110] See Statistisches Bundesamt (2009).

The publication of Kroll (2012) describes the ThyssenKrupp Steel Europe company, which has to handle the demographic change in its workforce with the additional challenge of having physical jobs and shift work. This company implemented a health shift program with the idea of offering a full day health seminar. The seminar takes place during working hours, so that all members of a shift participate. It contains lectures and workshops about health issues as well as individual health tests. A follow-up mentoring ensures the successful implementation of advice. The overall positive feedback of the participants combined with the mentoring affirms the effectiveness of the program in enhancing the working ability of the elderly.

Volunteering by the elderly might be regarded as a substitute for regular employment. The volunteering ratio, i.e., the share of volunteers within the population, of persons aged 50+ increased in general between 1999 and 2009. The highest increase in volunteering is of persons aged between 65 and 74, with 33% in 2009 compared to 19% in 1999. Several studies indicate that employment raises the probability of volunteering compared to unemployment or retirement. Further, higher education positively correlates with volunteering. Additionally, volunteers report a better health status than persons who do not participate in volunteering.[111] These three aspects might be interpreted in favor of volunteering. Hence, even at higher ages, volunteering seems rather a complement to than a substitute for employment. The majority of the elderly are willing to participate in society in an active way. More flexibility is not only preferred during the transition period between employment and retirement, but throughout an even larger period, where the elderly are still capable and active.[112]

Labor market policy has already started to react to the aging of the labor force. Several measures regarding the reemployment of individuals over 55 have been implemented in the past few years. There are clear differences between the labor market policy instruments for the elderly and for younger persons. Further, there are different focuses depending on whether the unemployed person belongs to SGB III or to

---

[111] See Dathe (2011).

[112] See Maxin and Deller (2010).

SGB II.[113] Within the regulation of SGB III instruments that support the beginning of employment dominate. The most common instruments are subsidies for the integration of the unemployed elderly into the workforce. On the other hand, instruments that create new employment opportunities are the focus within the regulation of SGB II. So-called "One-Euro-jobs" are the most used instruments for this purpose. The share of the elderly aged 55+ as participants in labor market policy instruments almost doubled between 2006 and 2011. A lag in the support of the unemployed older than 60 exists. Future labor market policy activities can try to resolve this.[114]

The OECD evaluates a multitude of states concerning their employment policies for dealing with aging and published the results in 2006. The report includes state-specific recommendations covering areas of financial incentives to promote employment, raise the employability of the elderly and overcome employers' employment obstacles. A follow-up report describes the actions taken and indicates aspects that remain unsolved. In general, almost all recommendations for Germany have been implemented, especially in regard to the better employability of the elderly. The only two remaining aspects are to monitor early retirement incentives and to promote best practices between social partners.[115] For the first aspect a possible action is proposed in chapter 5 of this thesis. The second might derive in the long run from that, since one of the main barriers to modern pro-aging employment policies are age limits or the retirement age.

Age limits are broadly accepted in German society as they structure the course of life to a great extent. The institutionalization of the life course has been one of the most fundamental developments in becoming a modern society.[116] Within the life course age limits concentrate on two periods: childhood and transition period into retirement. Legal capacity, liability, political participation, compulsory education and other aspects

---

[113] Unemployed persons who are entitled to unemployment insurance benefits are assigned to SGB III. In contrast, unemployed without an insurance claim and who are in need are assigned to SGB II. In 2012 68.9% of all unemployed were assigned to SGB II (see Bundesagentur für Arbeit).

[114] See Mümken and Brussig (2013).

[115] See OECD (2012b).

[116] See Kohli (1985).

are all linked to age limits and are aimed at protecting children by differentiating the life course. Age limits regarding retirement aim to protect the elderly from exhaustion. Further, third persons are also protected by age limits, e.g., adopted children from young adoptive parents who might be overstrained and not able yet to handle the responsibility, or patients from old doctors who might have a drawback in their capability due to age. Thus, both age limits can be seen as ability limits.[117]

Since age limits are derived from social processes, they are not predetermined but modifiable. In Germany, for example, majority was attained at the age of 21 until 1975 and then was lowered to 18 due to social progress.[118] At the beginning of social security the retirement age was set to 70, which was, at that time, an acceptable threshold to invalidity. Today, with a retirement age of 67, this justification no longer holds. As described in previous chapters, life expectancy is increasing constantly and also overall health is improving. On the other hand, capability verifiably declines only in part, accompanied by improvements in other relevant attributes. Moreover, further social progress is blurring the strict division between work and retirement. Life courses become more and more individual, leading to structural gaps if the elderly person is confronted with certain age regulations of the company, collective labor agreements or law.[119] Another function of age limits is the allocation of resources like labor and pension claims. Due to the demographic change, the potential of the elderly as human resource cannot be neglected. Further, maintaining the fairness of pension claims between cohorts is no longer achievable. Thus, also this argument no longer holds.[120]

Hence, there is a need for more flexibility in the labor market. Each party involved, whether employers, labor unions or the government, has to react to the changing needs and conditions that have already emerged and will arise in future.

---

[117] See Igl (2000).

[118] BGBl I 1713.

[119] See Riley et al. (1999).

[120] See Sackmann (2008) and Kohli (2000).

4 Contrasting retirement options in Germany

After having discussed the economic challenges of an aging society in chapter 2, chapter 3 elaborates recent developments and trends on three relevant fields, health, pension reforms and the labor market. All three have a great impact on the retirement decision of the individual. Based on these findings, the first research question of this thesis can be analyzed, namely:

What determines a delayed retirement? Why is this phenomenon so rare?

According to the facts elaborated so far, reasons of health can only be a justification in particular cases, since overall health of the population is continuously improving and a general decline appears later than the retirement age. Several positive effects derive from employment at higher ages, such as better social participation, a better self-reported health status and, at least, additional income. Planning to extend the employment period into higher ages, requires an understanding of individual retirement decisions. This chapter contrasts the retirement options in Germany, i.e., an early retirement versus a deferred retirement, as well as the motivations either against or in favor of each possibility. The aim is to point out significant determinants of the choice of the retirement date. In the next step, in chapter 5, an adequate modification of the pension system will be developed in order to answer the remaining, second research question.

4.1 Transition into retirement

An aging society challenges the funding of the pension scheme, particularly in the case of a pay-as-you-go system like the one in Germany. Increasing retiree-to-worker ratios are forcing politicians to adjust pension schemes. In Germany, this ratio is already above 50% and is expected to exceed 70% after 2030.[121] Besides cutting pension benefits, a

---

[121] See BMAS (2003).

reward for deferred retirement is being discussed.[122] While the first measure affects the elderly poverty rate in a negative way,[123] the second measure is mainly determined by actuarially fair concepts of pension system design. A third option is to raise the retirement age. In 2007, Germany raised the regular pension eligibility age from 65 stepwise to 67 for both women and men.[124] Intensified by the financial crisis and the poor current economic situation, many opponents complain about the bad employment opportunities of the elderly. Although the employment rate of older workers has increased in the last few years, they have difficulties keeping their jobs; at the same time older job-seekers face poor job prospects.[125] Since 57.9% of all pensions are drawn with deductions,[126] data from the statutory pension insurance (FDZ-RV) clearly demonstrates a bias towards early retirement. Would an amendment be able to change this general behavior? What actually determines the retirement decision?

Especially in Germany, the pathways to retirement are various. Table 5 shows the different paths to retirement for individuals born before 1964. The regular old-age pension makes up about 50% of all old-age pensions. Just over 20% are old-age pensions for women, followed by old-age pensions after unemployment and partial retirement with 13.7%. Pensions for general invalidity account for 10% of all pensions and pensions for long-standing insured account for about 8%.[127] Although the regular old–age pension eligibility age was 65, many individuals chose one of the early retirement opportunities. Accordingly, the mean age for claiming an old-age pension is generally lower than 65 and in 2010 it was 63.5.[128]

---

[122] See Keese et al. (2006).

[123] In Germany over 80% of the income of the elderly are public pensions. See Börsch-Supan (2009).

[124] RV-Altersgrenzenanpassungsgesetz (20.04.2007).

[125] See Keese et al. (2006).

[126] Rentenzugang 2010, Deutsche Rentenversicherung Bund (2011).

[127] Rentenversicherung in Zahlen 2010, Deutsche Rentenversicherung Bund.

[128] Rentenzugang 2010, Deutsche Rentenversicherung Bund (2011).

<table>
<tr><th></th><th>58</th><th>59</th><th>60</th><th>61</th><th>62</th><th>63</th><th>64</th><th>65</th><th>66</th><th>67</th></tr>
<tr><td>3 years of employment, 5 years of qualifying period</td><td colspan="7">pension due to limited earning capacity</td><td colspan="3">old-age pension</td></tr>
<tr><td>8 years of employment in the last 10 years, 15 years of qualifying period</td><td colspan="2">unemployment</td><td colspan="8">old-age pension after unemployment and partial retirement</td></tr>
<tr><td>8 years of employment in the last 10 years, 15 years of qualifying period</td><td colspan="2">partial retirement</td><td colspan="8">old-age pension after unemployment and partial retirement</td></tr>
<tr><td colspan="3">After the age of 40 10 years of contributions and 15 years of qualifying period</td><td colspan="8">old-age pension for women</td></tr>
<tr><td colspan="3">35 years of qualifying period</td><td colspan="8">old-age pension for general invalidity</td></tr>
<tr><td colspan="5">35 years of qualifying period</td><td colspan="6">old-age pension for long-standing insured</td></tr>
<tr><td colspan="8">5 years of qualifying period</td><td colspan="3">old-age pension</td></tr>
</table>

Source: own illustration based on Arnds and Bonin (2002).

Table 5: Pathways to retirement in Germany for individuals born before 1964

Two main theoretical approaches are used to explain the transition to retirement:[129]

i. *Pull factors*: from the microeconomic perspective a rational individual decides to retire when his/her utility starts to decrease while still employed. Therefore, early retirement derives from disincentives within the social security system. Estimations based on an option value model underlie the hypothesis, that a higher option value diminishes the risk of retiring early.[130]

ii. *Push factors*: the individual has no significant influence on the retirement decision, however, external factors like the labor market or serious health issues determine the exit time. The retirement decision in this situation is involuntary to some extent.[131]

---

[129] See Radl (2007).

[130] See Antolin and Scarpetta (1998).

[131] See Szinovacz and Davey (2005).

Besides these factors mentioned above, sociological factors affecting retirement age are also discussed in the literature. The idea is that the individual lifecycle follows a symbolic trisection (i.e. childhood, occupation and retirement) with sociologically determined transitions in between.[132] The present study is concerned with the pull and push factors of retirement. The focus of previous studies was either on the impact that pull and push factors have on early retirement or on deferred retirement. This study is the first to analyze the effect of these factors on both early and deferred retirement in a unified framework. Intuitively, factors that impact an early retirement might be supposed to have the opposite effect on deferred retirement. For example, if lower education correlates positively with early retirement, a bigger proportion of lower educated persons will be observed within the group of early retirees. What conclusions concerning a deferred retirement can be drawn from? More precisely, does higher education automatically correlate negative with early retirement? Or, does higher education as a result positively correlate with deferred retirement? I will investigate these coherences in the following study of this chapter. First, I will give an overview over the current state of research on this topic. In contrast to my intention, the research published so far concentrates on the effects of either early retirement or on deferred retirement.

Debrand and Sirven (2009) looked at the determinants of the pathways to early retirement in Europe. Their results indicate that various variables, such as employment, workplace conditions, disability, health status, education, household structure and the spouse's occupation affect the retirement decision. However, these determinants are not sufficient to explain the observable differences in retirement age in Europe. The authors' conclude that these differences can best be explained by the specific characteristics of the social security systems of the respective European countries.

Hoffman (2007) studied the multiple factors that play a role in early retirement in Germany. The author found that, in general, higher educated and qualified persons stay employed longer and therefore retire later.[133] In particular, a high percentage of early retirement can be observed in the group of individuals who are unemployed for a

---

[132] See Behrens and Voges (1996).

[133] See also other authors like Clemens et al. (2007) and Radl (2006).

longer time just before retirement.[134] However, a monotonic dependency between education, profession and income and the retirement age could not be proved.[135]

Brussig (2010b, 2010c) examined the increase in the employment rate in Germany for persons aged 55+, which has been continuous since 2000, as well as the contemporaneous increase in part-time employment for this age group and identified a cohort effect. The findings showed that individuals of younger cohorts (aged 55-59) are employed longer than individuals in older cohorts (aged 60-64). Moreover, in younger cohorts, the employment rate for women is higher while the absolute size of the cohort is smaller. Thus, the decline in the labor market exit age does not contradict the positive trend of the employment rate of older workers due to the disproportionate sizes of the different cohorts. In a later study, Brussig (2010d) identified the kind of jobs that are still performed after the age of 60. Simple service providers, as well as managers, are more likely to work past the age of 60. In contrast, employees in manual professions are more likely to stop working earlier. Beyond the regular pension eligibility age, the job of simple service provider is dominant.

With respect to Germany, the effect that an increase in the pension eligibility age has on the expected retirement age was analyzed by Coppola and Wilke (2010). Higher educated workers seem to be encouraged to retire later. Women, on the other hand, are less willing to wait until the regular pension eligibility and usually opt for early retirement. Less productive workers also tend to retire earlier if they belong to rather well-off households.

Montalto et al. (2000) addressed the question of whether the individual's age has an impact on the planned retirement age. Their results suggest that planned retirement age rises over the individual's lifetime.

Riphahn and Schmidt (2007) analyzed the influence that the incentives set by the German public pension system have on retirement age and provide evidence that individuals systematically react to these incentives. They also considered

[134] See Brussig (2010a).

[135] See Radl (2006) and Berkel and Börsch-Supan (2006).

unemployment rates and found that unemployment has no significant influence on the decision to retire early.

Himmelreicher et al. (2009) focused on the effect that the level of education has on retirement age in Germany. Based on data from the public pension system of 2006, these authors confirmed the hypothesis that education positively affects retirement age. Within the group of early retirees, as well as overall, higher educated persons have a higher retirement age of about one year on average. Even though the duration of employment is shorter in total, higher educated individuals are able to acquire higher pensions. Therefore, they often retire early and take a loss in their pension level in favor of leisure. Astleither et al. (2010) confirmed these results. Furthermore, they provided evidence of a time trend leading to an increase in retirement age over time.

Siegrist et al. (2006) found that poor health has a negative impact on the intention to continue working. The incentive to retire early for a person with health problems is the prospect of improvement when retired. However, as Börsch-Supan and Jürges (2007) pointed out, the improvement must not necessarily imply a better health status, but greater well-being in general.

Arnds and Bonin (2002), Budimir (2007), Widmer (2003) and Radl (2007) investigated the income effect of early retirement. The income effect addresses the issue of whether higher income individuals or wealthier individuals can afford more leisure and therefore retire earlier. Theoretically, no definite conclusion could be drawn since higher income and wealthier individuals typically receive higher wages, which means that they face higher opportunity costs with early retirement. The results of Budimir (2007), Widmer (2003) and Radl (2007) suggest that higher income and wealthier individuals are more reluctant to retire early. Arnds and Bonin (2002), however, expect that the income effect will become more important in the future.

The only empirical study I am aware of that considers deferred retirement in Germany is the one by Piekkola and Deschryvere (2005). These authors showed that well-being at work and good health are the most effective factors in explaining deferred retirement.

The aim of this chapter is to consider the determinants of early and deferred retirement in a unified framework. The underlying idea is that the same factors that determine early retirement also determine deferred retirement, but with the opposite sign. If this is the case, the lessons that can be drawn from the evidence on early retirement, can contribute to an understanding of how to encourage individuals to work longer. I discuss this in the next four sections. Section 4.2 formulates the main hypotheses underlying this empirical analysis, describes the data set and provides descriptive statistics on early and deferred retirement. Section 4.3 establishes a multiple logistic regression model. Section 4.4 discusses the results and Section 4.5 concludes.

4.2 Hypotheses and data

In line with the results of previous literature I make the following two hypotheses.

Hypothesis 1: *The retirement decision is determined by push factors, as well as by the social, educational and economic attributes of the individual.*

Hypothesis 2: *Early and deferred retirement are determined by the same factors with opposite sign.*

The data used to study these hypotheses is taken from the third wave of the Deutscher Alterssurvey (DEAS) from 2008.[136] This is a representative nationwide cross-sectional survey of individuals in the second half of their lives (40-85 years old). The interviews took place between April 2008 and November 2008, mainly at home of the respondents and last 90 min on average. The survey also includes 6,205 new interviews with individuals regarding their life situation. The method used for collecting the data was a Computer Assisted Personal Interview. Additionally, an optional self-completion questionnaire was part of the survey, which mainly includes information concerning the individual's financial situation. Since this information is an important aspect of the analysis, respondents who did not complete the optional self-completion questionnaire are dropped out. As the focus of the study is on the retirement decision, only those persons who are already retired were considered for the analysis. Also pensions for widows and orphans, as well as pensions due to limited earning capacity, are excluded. Furthermore, individuals who stated a retirement age of below 55 were excluded from

---

[136] See Kröger et al. (2011) for more details on this data set and a discussion of alternative data sets.

the analysis.[137] The reason for the last exclusion is that there is no pathway to retirement below the age of 55 apart from pension schemes for orphans' and widows' and pensions due to limited earning capacity. This resulted in 2,014 observations considered for the analysis.

Table 6 gives a brief overview of the basic structure of the data. Males are overrepresented in this sample with 58.19%.[138] The retirement ages vary between 55 and 75 with a median of 61. Only a small fraction of the retirees of 6.45% is still employed.

Attributes	Sample 2008 retirees 55+
Total number of cases	2,014
Gender	
male	1,172
female	842
Age[139]	
median	71
minimum	60
maximum	85
Employed	130
Retirement age	
median	61
minimum	55
maximum	75

Table 6: Characteristics of the third wave of DEAS in 2008

[137] This applies to 4.1% of the sample.

[138] In contrast, pursuant to official data of the German Pension Insurance only 44.18% of the recipients of old-age pensions were male by 31.12.2008.

[139] Refers to the age of the individual at the time of the interview.

Figure 17 shows the year of birth and the retirement age distribution of the sample. The median age is 71. The results of the survey show that 10.1% retire under the age of 60, most individuals retire between the ages of 60 and 64 (65.4%) and 20.8% retire at the regular pension eligibility age of 65. Only a small percentage of individuals (3.8%) retire with an age older than 65.

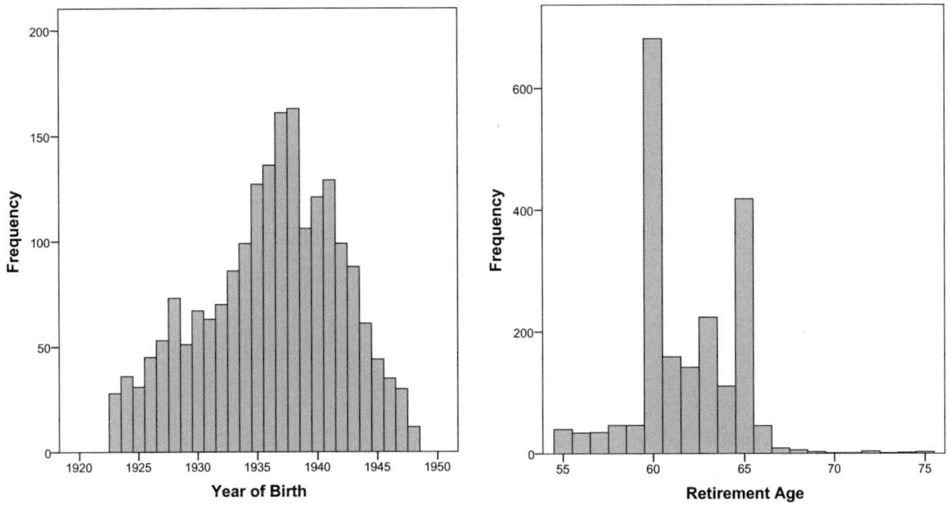

Source: own calculations.

Figure 17: Histograms of the year of birth and retirement age

The years of birth range from 1923 to 1948. Thus, the earliest that the participants could claim their pensions was in 1978 or later. During this period, several reforms of the pension system took place, which resulted in changes to the pension eligibility age.[140] Therefore, for each cohort of individuals, the pension eligibility age was considered according to the regulations that applied to this cohort. More precisely, I conduct a cohort specific classification and assure comparability despite different age limits. Thus, Individuals who retired at the regular pension eligibility age received their own old-age pension without any reductions, whereas the pensions of individuals who retired earlier included a deduction and the pensions of individuals who had deferred retirement included a bonus.[141]

[140] Changes mainly due to the Rentenreformgesetz 1992.

[141] See SGB VI Anlage 19, 20, 21, 22.

Figure 18 illustrates the situation after applying the pension eligibility age individually valid for a certain cohort. A trend towards early retirement can be observed. The younger the retirees are, the higher the percentage of individuals who choose early retirement. Clearly, individuals born in 1943 or later had not yet reached the pension eligibility age of 65 in 2008, therefore these individuals belong to the group of early retirees (see the last four bars in Figure 18).

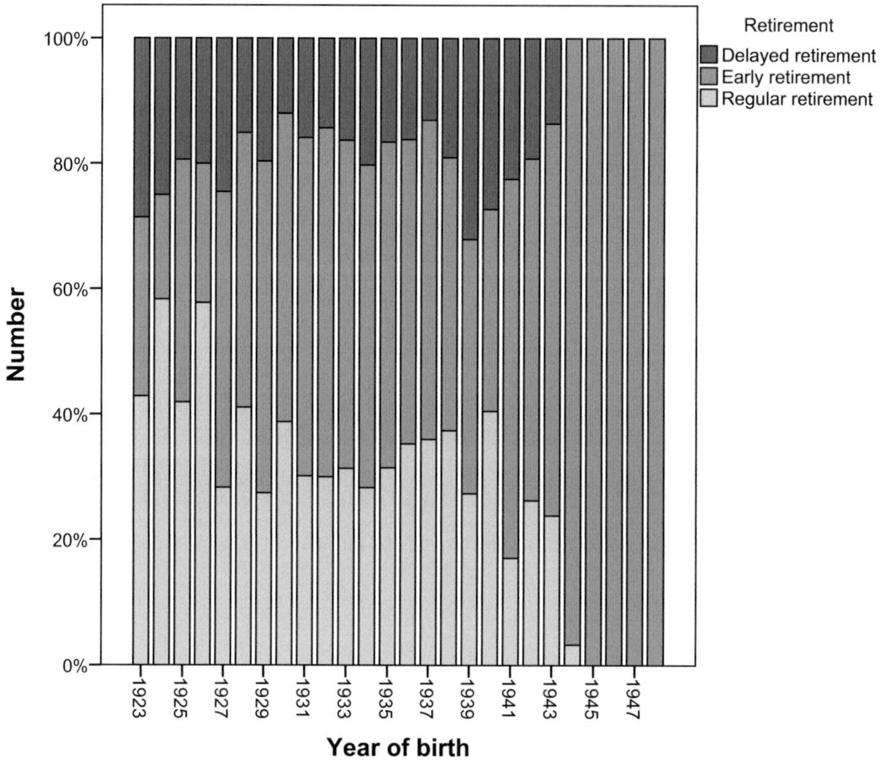

Source: own calculations.

Figure 18: Retirement classes of participants by year of birth

4.3 Descriptive statistics

The survey includes an explicit question on the reasons that led to the termination of the last employment. Figure 19 shows the variety of motives for ultimately leaving the labor force. Although multiple responses were possible, the mean number of responses was only 1.18. It seems that the majority left the labor force for a single reason. The main reason was that the individual had reached the first possible pension eligibility age. This was stated by 46% of the respondents. 20% left for operational reasons, another 8.2% became unemployed. 17.5% retired because of poor health conditions. Even though the data set does not include pensions due to limited earning capacity or pensions for invalid persons, the number of persons who were not able to continue working because of poor health is relatively high. Only 6.7% stated that they wanted to stop working as early as possible. Retirement of the partner was given as a reason by 1.4%, therefore the joint retirement hypothesis[142], which assumes that husbands and wives tend to retire coordinate their retirement, is not supported by the descriptive data.

In evaluating the statements on the termination of the last employment separately for the three different groups of retirees, some differences become apparent. Early retirees stated operational and health reasons twice as often as persons who retired at the regular retirement age. This may indicate that early retirement was involuntary. Persons who defer their retirement give family reasons five times as often as regular retirees and twice as often as individuals who cite having to care for another person. The remaining reasons do not differ significantly between the groups.

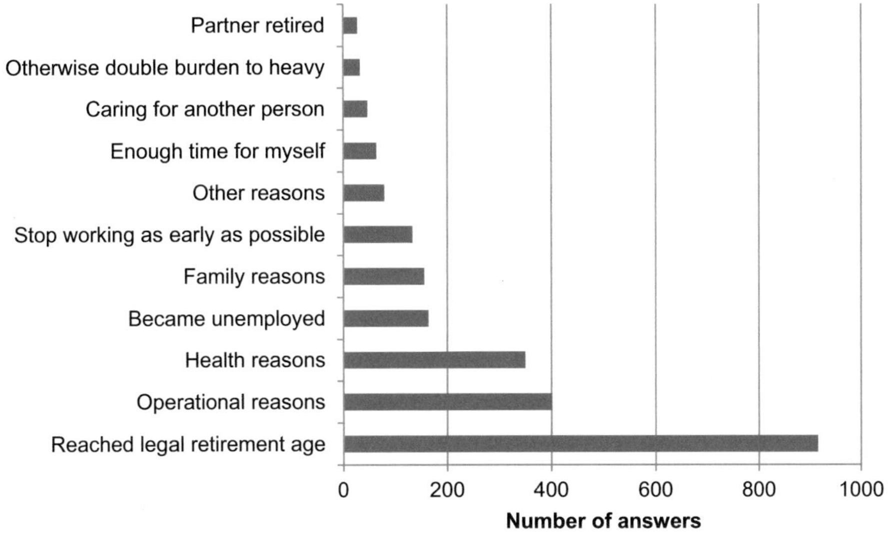

Source: own calculations.

Figure 19: Reasons for termination of employment

[142] See Hurd (1990).

An interesting group of retirees are the ones, that are still employed, but who are already drawing their old-age pension. The data set contains 130 of these individuals (6.5%).[143] They were explicitly asked why they want to continue working. Figure 20 shows the different answers given. Again, multiple answers were possible. The mean number of answers was 2.12, so there were generally two reasons mentioned per person. While for over 70% of the respondents fun at work was a motivation to continue working, contact to other people (47.7%), as well as still having a task (44.6%), were also important factors. Financial reasons were stated by 35.4%.

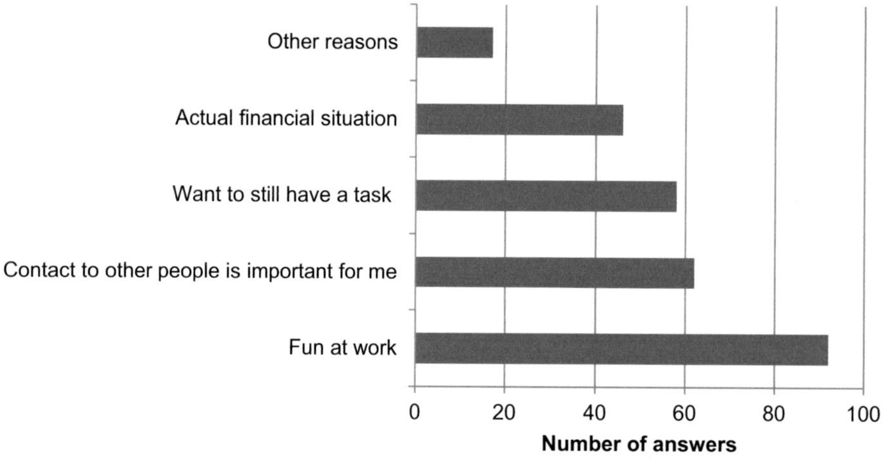

Source: own calculations.

Figure 20: Reasons for being employed as a retiree

The correlation between the health status and employment at higher ages seeks for being evaluated more detailed. Over 17% of the respondents stated health reasons as main reason to exit the labor market. Consequently, the data should provide measurable differences in the health status between retirees who are employed and retirees who are not employed. As it is one of the main ambitions of this thesis to motivate the elderly to remain longer in employment, the interaction of health and employment deserves further study.

143 An actual report on older people in Germany based on data from the European Labor Force Survey verifies this number, stating that 6% of persons aged 65-74 are employed (see Statistisches Bundesamt (2011)).

The data set contains several health variables, mostly based on individual self-evaluations. Physical functioning is measured by the according subscale of the SF-36 Health Survey[144]. Hereby, the extent of physical impairment of ten activities is measured. Each of the every-day activities, like ascending stairs or bending down, is evaluated on a three stage scale from "strongly limited" to "no limitation at all". The scale is directly transformed into a 0-100 scale, so that high values of this variable correspond to a good physical functioning. Although not considering the quality of sleep, the SF-36 is international broadly accepted as a self-evaluation measurement of health-related quality of life. Further, it is also proper for an application to the elderly.[145]

The evaluation of the SF-36 variable, by controlling for being employed as a retiree, leads to 129 cases with a mean value of 87.02 points and a standard deviation of 18.26. The median is 95 points, which means that more than the half (i.e. 70.5%) of all cases achieve rather high values of 95 points at minimum. Currently, almost 30% achieve the highest possible value of 100 points. The mean value is lower at 78.42 points with a standard deviation of 24.29 in the group of retirees who are not employed (1,878 cases). The median is 90 points. In this group at least 19.4% achieve the maximum possible value of 100 points. It becomes apparent that the group of retirees who still have an employment achieve higher values in the SF-36 health survey combined with a lower standard deviation. Thus, this group is more homogeny and has a better health status than retirees who are not employed as can be seen from Figure 21. Nevertheless, the difference is quite small and, further, concentrates at high values (between 80 and 100 points).

---

[144] See Bulliger and Kirchberger (1998).

[145] See Gunzelmann et al. (2006).

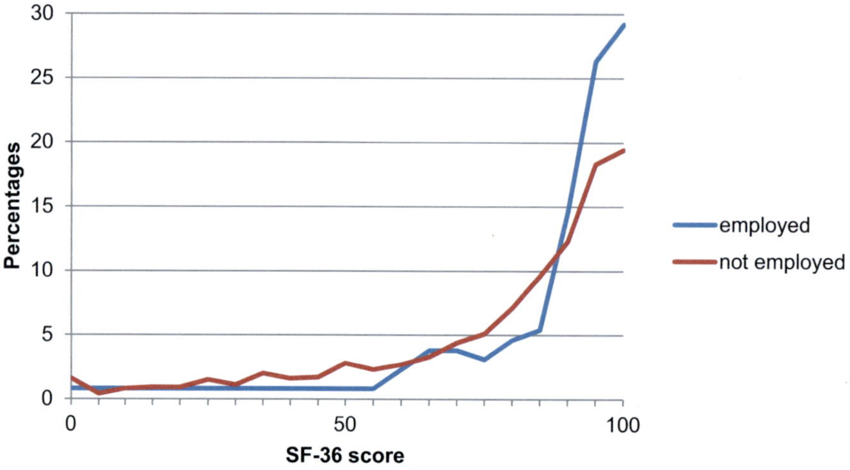

Source: own calculations.

Figure 21: Frequency distribution of the SF-36 score of retirees

As the SF-36 is based on self-evaluation of the individuals, I analyze another health variable that is a bit more objective. The respondents had been asked about current several physical diseases (each can be answered by yes or no). I create a new variable "*number of physical diseases*" which counts the number of positive answers according to the twelve options[146] plus two open options, which can be filled with other diseases. Again, I distinguish between retirees who are employed and retirees who are not. The first group has 130 valid cases and shows a mean value of 2.68 physical diseases with a standard deviation of 2.15. The median is 2 physical diseases. The mean value is higher in the group of retirees without an employment. So, the mean value is 3.13 physical diseases with a standard deviation of 2.09, which is almost the same value compared to the other group. Though, the median is about one disease higher at three. Nonetheless, 10.3% of all retirees without employment stated to have no physical diseases at all. Within the group of employed retirees 14.6% did so, which is more, indeed, but again not as much as might be expected. Figure 22 shows the two different profiles regarding the number of diseases. Obviously, a greater share of employed retirees has only two or

[146] The twelve listed physical diseases are: cardiovascular diseases; circulatory disorder; joint, bone, intervertebral disks or back ailments; dyspnea, asthma or respiratory diseases; gastro-intestinal diseases; cancer; diabetes; bile, liver or nephritic ailments; bladder ailments; insomnia; impaired vision or eye complaints; deafness or ear complaints.

less physical diseases compared to retirees without employment. On the contrary, in the area between four and nine diseases the share of retirees who are not employed is higher.

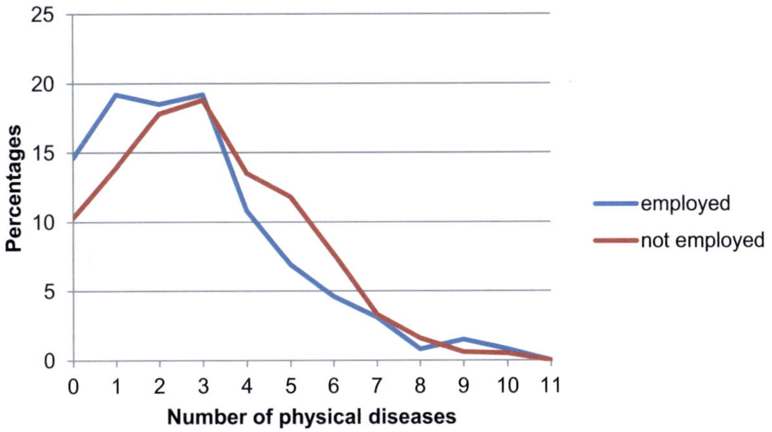

Source: own calculations.

Figure 22: Frequency distribution of the number of physical diseases of retirees

In order to derive a general assumption out of these findings, the different structure of both groups has to be taken into account. Thus, gender as well as age structure is quite different. Both had been verified to influence the health status of the individual. Regarding the SF-36, an age effect arises in almost all subscales including the subscale of physical functioning.[147] Further, men tend to be better off than women in five out of eight subscales.[148] Whereas the group of unemployed retirees is quite balanced in gender (57.6% are males), the group of employed retirees is dominated by males with 66.9%. Here the good health results are caused to some extend by gender. The majority of the group of employed retirees is younger than 75 and only 13.1% are older than 75 years. On the contrary, within the group of retirees without an employment 31.1% are older than 75. In general, the subjective health status as well as physical functioning declines with age. Thus, it might be the case that the numerous younger retirees within the group of employed retirees bias the results towards a better health status on

[147] Solely the subscales mental health and social role do not differ significantly between age groups. (See Gunzelmann et al. (2006)).

[148] The subscales social role, physical role and emotional role show no differences between genders. (See Gunzelmann et al. (2006)).

average. Therefore, I evaluate both variables regarding the health status, after having divided the data again into several age groups. The outcomes do not differ significantly for all age groups. Thus, despite the age of the individuals, the health status of employed retirees is better than for retirees who are not employed on average.

The interdependence between health status and employment status of retirees can work in both directions. Either a good health status of the retirees allows for an ongoing employment, or the employment itself supports a better health status of the retiree. While many politicians and labor unions often argue in favor of the first direction, academic literature provides evidence for the latter.[149] So far, my analysis shows a positive correlation between a good health status and an employment, but the direction of action is not clear. Therefore, I further divide the group of retirees without an employment relative to their intention to take up employment, as the respondents had been explicitly asked about that. Only 45 retirees had stated to have the intention to take up an employment. Due to the small number of cases, the corresponding graphs in Figure 23 and Figure 24 are erratic.

Figure 23 is based on Figure 21 but distinguishes the not employed retirees between those without the intention to take up employment, and those having the intention to take up employment. It can be seen, that lower score numbers (i.e. a score number below 35) are not represented at all within the group of retirees with the intention. At the same time, the maximum score of 100 occurs more often in this group in comparison to the group without the intention. Accordingly, the mean value for the latter group is 78.22, which is about 8 points lower compared to the group with an intention to take up employment (86.49). Moreover, the standard deviation of 24.44 is about 35% higher than the standard deviation of the retirees who are not willing to take up an employment (15.95). After including the group of employed retirees, this group performs the best (mean value: 87.02; standard deviation: 18.26).

---

[149] For example Zhan et al. (2009) show that bridge employment is beneficial for the health status of retirees.

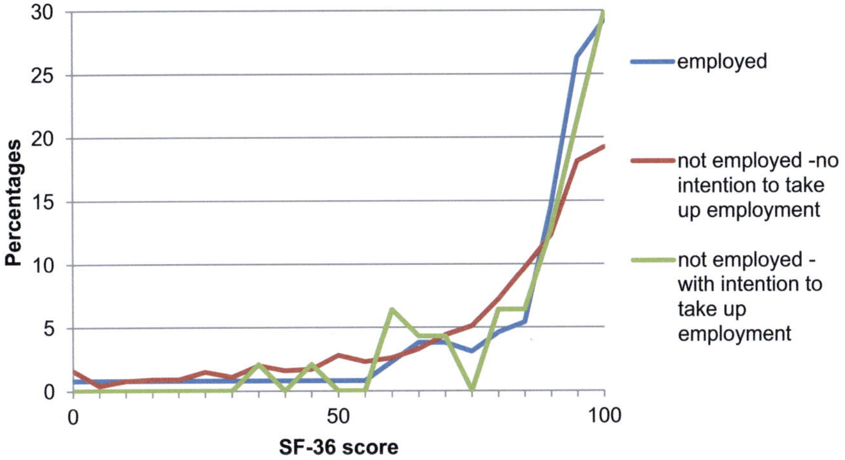

Source: own calculations.

Figure 23: Frequency distribution of the SF-36 score of retirees specified

Figure 24 is based on Figure 22 but, again, differentiates between the not employed retirees without the intention to take up employment, and those having the intention to take up employment. These two subgroups have quite similar results. The mean value of the number of physical diseases is 3.13, which is identical for both subgroups. The standard deviation is a bit higher for the group without the intention to take up an employment (2.1 compared to 1.87). Overall, the group of employed retirees has the lowest mean value of 2.68 at a standard deviation of 2.15.

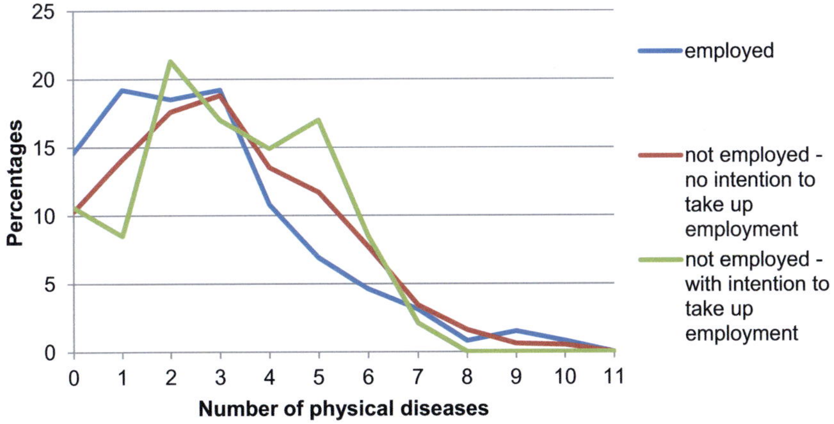

Source: own calculations.

Figure 24: Frequency distribution of the number of physical diseases of retirees specified

In general, the health status of employed retirees is better than the health status of retirees without an employment. Nevertheless, the differences in health status are moderate. After having separated of the unemployed retirees by the intention to take up an employment or not, the differences in the health status diminish even further. While physical functioning, which is measured by the SF-36 score, shows higher and thus better values for the subgroup who wants to take up an employment, the number of physical diseases does not differ on average. Notably, among the group of retirees wanting to work, about 28% currently have five or more physical diseases. Moreover, even some retirees with a SF-36 score below 50 are willing to take up an employment. On the other hand, only 3.8% of the unemployed retirees with the maximum score of 100 points show the willingness to work.

Hence, an interdependence between the health status and an employment as retiree exist, but the direction of action is not one way but rather opposed. A good health status is not a mandatory precondition to take up an employment as retiree, however, it affects stimulating.

4.4 The model

I employed a multiple logistic regression model to study the hypotheses. A multiple logistic regression model is a generalization of the binary logistic model.[150] Parameter estimations are based on an iterative maximum likelihood algorithm. It is assumed that the odds ratios of any two categories are independent of all the other response categories. Also, given a covariate pattern, the responses are assumed to be independent multinomial variables.

The dependent variable Y_i , $i \in \{1, \dots, c\}$, has several categories and is nominally scaled. Furthermore, there are several independent variables x_i. The probability of occurrence of category r is

[150] See Fahrmeier et al. (2009), p. 238ff.

$$P(Y_i = r \mid x_i) = \pi_i = \frac{\exp(x_i' \beta_r)}{1 + \sum_{s=1}^{q} \exp(x_i' \beta_s)} \qquad r = 1, \dots, q.$$

For the reference category c

$$\pi_{ic} = 1 - \pi_{i1} - \dots - \pi_{iq} = \frac{1}{1 + \sum_{s=1}^{q} \exp(x_i' \beta_s)}$$

holds. Equivalent to this is

$$log \frac{\pi_{ir}}{\pi_{ic}} = x_i' \beta_r \qquad r = 1, \dots, c.$$

The parameters $\beta_r = (\beta_{r0}, \beta_{r1}, \dots, \beta_{rk})'$ and the predictors $\mu_{ir} = x_i' \beta_r = \beta_{ro} + x_{i1}\beta_{r1} + \dots + x_{ik}\beta_{rk}, r = 1, \dots, q$, are specific for each category.

This exponential multiplicative model specifies the odds ratio between the category r and c as the reference category using the predictor $\mu_{ir} = x_i' \beta_r$ by modeling the logits for the relation between the categories r $(Y = r)$ and c $(Y = c)$.

Brussig (2006), Lund (2005) and Pozzebon (1989) use binary logistic regression models. Since this study considers three different possible choices (early, regular, deferred retirement) a multiple logistic regression is necessary.[151]

By categorizing the determinants (listed in Table 7) into socio-demographic characteristics, socio-economic characteristics and employment characteristics, three multiple logistic regressions were conducted to study both hypotheses.

---

[151] Another possible approach used e.g. by Radl (2007), Piekkola and Deschryvere (2005) and Bütler et al. (2004) is to model retirement as a probability of survival (by hazard functions) and then use duration models.

Variable	Label	Values	# valid cases	Median	Min	Max	Std. deviation
Socio-demographic characteristics:							
gen**	gender	1 = female, 2 = male	2,014	1	1	2	0.493
nchild	number of children	1 = no children, 2 = one child, 3 = two children, 4 = three children, 5 = four children, 6 = five or more children	2,010	3	1	6	1.205
edu	education	1 = high qualified, 2 = middle qualified, 3 = low qualified, 4 = no qualification	1,936	3	1	4	0.792
mart**	marital status	1 = married/registered partnership, 2 = divorced/separated, 3 = widowed, 4 = single	2,011	1	1	4	1.349
reg**	region	1 = West Germany, 2 = East Germany	2,014	1	1	2	0.486
Employment characteristics:							
ecosec**	economic sector	1 = agricultural, 2 = industry, 3 = trade, 4 = commerce , 5 = public sector	1,789	4	1	5	1.250
comsiz**	company size	1 = less than 5 employees, 2 = 5 - 19 employees, 3 = 20 - 99 employees, 4 = 100 - 199 employees, 5 = 200 – 1,999 employees, 6 = 2,000 or more employees	1,717	3	1	6	1.577
prof**	profession	1 = farmer, 2 = academic, 3 = helping family, 4 = self-employed, 5 = civil servant, 6 = clerk, 7 = worker	1,993	6	1	7	1.240
emp*	dummy variable employed	0 = no, 1 = yes	2,013	0	0	1	0.246
jint**	total years of job interruption	1 = 0 years, 2 = 1-2 years, 3 = 3-5 years, 4 = 6-60 years	2,007	1	1	3	1.016
sbret**	situation before retirement	1 = employed, 2 = partial retirement (released phase), 3 = unemployed, 4 = preretirement, 5 = disability pension/long-term sickness, 6 = house wife/man	1,960	1	1	6	1.667
Socio-economic characteristics:							
hincg**	household income group (€/month)	1 = 0 – 1,500; 2 = 1,501 – 3,000; 3 = 3,001 – 4,500; 4 = > 4,500	1,847	2	1	4	0.794
asset**	amount of total assets	1 = no assets at all; 2 = up to 25,000; 3 = 25,001 – 100,000; 4 = more than 100,000	1,773	2	1	4	0.872
save**	dummy variable savings	0 = no, 1 = yes	1,929	1	0	1	0.500
open**	pension (€/month)	1 = up to 850; 2 = 851 – 1,250; 3 = more than 1250	1,537	2	1	3	0.820
penhw**	pension husband/wife (€/month)	1 = up to 850; 2 = 851 – 1,250; 3 = more than 1250	922	1	1	3	0.784

** = Chi-squared test with p-value below 0.05.

* = Chi-squared test with p-value below 0.1.

Table 7: List of independent variables

4.5 Results

Model 1 only contains socio-demographic characteristics (Nagelkerke-R^2 = 0.330).[152] By adding stepwise employment characteristics (Model 2) and socio-economic characteristics (Model 3), the Nagelkerke-R^2 value increases to 0.511. Hence, in Model 3 at least half of the variance of the dependent variable can be explained with the independent ones.

	Early retirement			*Deferred retirement*		
Odds ratio for a contrast	Model 1	Model 2	Model 3	Model 1	Model 2	Model 3
female to male	4.118***	4.864***	4.757***	0.160***	0.290***	
West to East Germany	1.941***	2.727***	3.868***	4.718***	2.699***	2.222*
high level to no level of education			6.271*	3.430*		
middle level to no level of education			12.084**			
low level to no level of education			8.784**			
one child to five or more	1.682*					
economic sector: agricultural to public sector		0.532**				
company size: < 5 employees to 2.000+		0.580*				
company size: 20-99 employees to 2,000+			0.522*			
company size: 200-1,999 employees to 2,000+		0.632*	0.480**			
profession: helping family to worker					8.167**	
profession: self-employed to worker			11.817*			

[152] The Nagelkerke-R^2 can reach a maximum value of 1 and therefore be interpreted clearly. Values above 0.2 are acceptable, values above 0.4 are good and values above 0.5 are very good (See Backhaus, 2011, p. 449ff.).

profession: clerk to worker		0.700**	0.432***			
situation before retirement: employed to house wife/man					0.170***	0.221***
situation before retirement: partial retirement to house wife/man		4.237***	5.924**		0.127***	
situation before retirement: unemployed to house wife/man		4.796***	8.261***		0.106***	0.177**
situation before retirement: preretirement to house wife/man					0.128***	
situation before retirement: disability pension/long-term sickness to house wife/man					0.150***	0.556**
no job interruption to 6 years or more		2.080**	2.199*			
1-2 years job interruption to 6 years or more			2.604*			
up to €850 own pension to more than €1,250						4.586**
up to €850 pension husband/wife to more than €1,250						0.307*
€851-€1,250 pension husband/wife to more than €1,250						0.332**

* = p-value < 0.1;
** = p-value < 0.05;
*** = p-value < 0.01

Table 8: Significant odds ratios

In order to reduce endogeneity, the individual pension amount was adjusted to the regular old-age pension amount without any reductions or bonuses. Doing so this variable became more comparable and further is independent of the individual retirement time.

Table 8 presents all significant odds ratios for all three regression models.[153] The first column contains the attributes that are compared. The corresponding odds ratios for early retirement are listed in the second column and for deferred retirement they are

[153] The complete table including all regression results is attached in the appendix.

listed in the third column. For the purpose of clarity, insignificant results are omitted. Apparently, only few characteristics are significant for both retirement options. In fact, socio-demographic and some employment characteristics are dominant for early retirement, while the situation just before retirement and economic aspects are decisive for deferred retirement. By extending the model the significance of some attributes changes. Moreover, there are new characteristics which are significant in the extended version of Model 3. At the same time, some other characteristics become insignificant. The values do not change drastically. In the following, the results of Model 3 are discussed in detail. The reference group for all of the evaluations is always retirement at regular retirement age.

Socio-demographic characteristics:

The probability of a woman (compared to a man) retiring early is much higher (odds ratio = 4.757). This is a well-known phenomenon because of the typical employment history of women in these cohorts and the fact that they can draw a special old-age pension for women (see Table 4). In contrast, deferring retirement is not significantly influenced by gender. Region has a significant influence on both early retirement and deferred retirement. West Germans are more likely to retire earlier than East Germans (odds ratio = 3.868). At the same time, the probability of deferring retirement is also higher for West Germans than for East Germans (odds ratio = 2.222).[154] While previous literature supports the latter, the first tendency is contradictory to the literature. The level of education determines the probability of early retirement. Compared to having no qualifications at all, higher qualifications increase the probability to retire early, whereby individuals with middle qualifications have the highest odds ratio (12.084). Thus, a linear relationship between early retirement and level of education does not exist. In fact, the chance to retire early is twice as high for middle educated persons as for higher educated persons and one third higher than for lower educated. However, there is no significant correlation between deferred retirement and education. The number of children or marital status does not influence the time of retirement either negatively or positively, therefore no conclusions can be drawn.

---

[154] Significance level of 10%.

Although the health status has been considered, no significant influences within the regression could be detected.[155] Therefore, a more detailed descriptive evaluation of the interdependency between the health status and an employment as retiree was conducted in Chapter 4.3. To recap, employed retirees have a better health status on average, albeit the differences were moderate referred to the unemployed retirees. Some individuals with a poor health status exists among the group of employed retirees, as well as some individuals with excellent health status exist within the group of unemployed retirees without the intention to take up an employment. Further, the direction of influence is ambiguous. Thus, the health status is not the major determinant for the employment decision. Especially, since the data involves only normal old-age pension and no invalidity pensions or pensions due to limited earning capacity, the influence of health should be rather limited.[156] A definition of well-being would be more convenient for this purpose. Hereby, the individuals tend to reassess their subjective evaluation of their health status as well as well-being relative to the performance of comparable persons around him. However, the data does not provide any information on this.

Employment characteristics:

Within the group of employment characteristics, the economic sector is not significant.[157] Working at a company with fewer than 2,000 employees reduces the likelihood of early retirement by 0.480 (for a company with 200 – 1,999 employees) or by 0.522[158] for a company with 20 – 99 employees. The reason for this might be a stronger personal relationship between employees as well as the better individual

---

[155] Several self-assessments of the retirees have been taken into account. So, the respondents were asked about their recent health status. Their answers were as follows: very good (5.9%), good (39.7%), middle (41.4%), bad (10.3%) and very bad (2.7%). Additionally, the SF-36 variable as well as the number of current physical diseases was tested.

[156] Antolin and Scarpetta (1998) found that there is a positive correlation between claiming a pension for disabled persons or a pension due to limited earning capacity and poor health status. However, for other forms of pensions, they do not identify a significant influence.

[157] Only in Model 2 do employees from the agricultural sector tend to retire early more often compared to employees from the public sector.

[158] Significance level of 10%.

working conditions in smaller firms. Compared to a worker, a clerk is less likely to retire early (odds ratio = 0.432). Self-employed individuals favor early retirement much more than workers (odds ratio = 11.817). A sufficient income and general wealth might be the reason for this finding. An employment after retirement has no significant effect on the retirement decision. It could be that the decision to work as a retiree is made after retirement and therefore does not affect the retirement decision. It is self-evident that partial retirement enhances the chance to retire early compared to a housewife/-man. Furthermore, individuals who were housewives/-men just before their retirement but who have gained sufficient claims in the past are less prone to retire early than individuals who were unemployed. The odds ratio of deferred retirement is higher for housewives/-men, respectively. Being a housewife/-man might indicate that the husband or wife earns enough for both of them, so there is no need to accept a reduction in the pension amount in order to get one's own pension as early as possible. Having a job even diminishes the chance of deferring retirement. In contrast, the total years of job interruption does not seem to be a determinant for deferring retirement. Individuals with a job interruption of zero to two years have a higher odds ratio of early retirement compared to individuals with a job interruption of more than 6 years. The underlying reason may be that individuals with more years of work will receive a higher pension. Therefore they may prefer having more leisure time in the form of earlier retirement.

Socio economic characteristics:

While socio economic characteristics, like household income, total amount of assets or savings have no significant impact, either on early retirement or deferred retirement, having one's own pension, as well as the pension of the husband/wife influences the decision to take deferred retirement. An own pension below €850 increases the chance of taking late retirement by 4.5 compared to individuals with a pension of more than €1,250. Thus, a rather low pension level forces the individual to defer retirement in order to achieve the pension bonus for a higher pension level in future. Conversely, retirees with a husband or wife with a pension of no more than €1,250 are less likely (odds ratio = 0.307 and 0.332) to defer their own retirement compared to individuals with a husband or wife receiving a pension of more than €1,250. Again, a possible reason may be the economic situation of the couple as a whole, both together representing one household. Presumably, the individual is not forced to claim his own pension but is somehow financed by the partner. This enables the chance of defer the own retirement and achieve the bonus in the own pension.

Overall, the classification of the regression increases from 63.3% (Model 1) to 71.6% (Model 3).[159] Especially for the early retirement group, the classifications of the models are very high with a maximum value of 86.9% in Model 3. Nearly 50% are matched accurately to the group of regular retirement. For both groups, the percentage share increases from Model 1 to Model 3. The classification of deferred retirees is quite good in Model 1 (67.8%). The percentage share drops to 50.6% in Model 2 and increases to 53.2% in Model 3. However, the number of cases evaluated within the models decreases. The reason for this is the inclusion of the additional financial information requested in the optional self-completion questionnaire, which was not fully completed by all the participants. Nevertheless, a sufficient number of cases are always attained for a logistic regression.[160]

4.6 Concluding remarks

Early retirement can be mostly explained by socio-demographic and employment characteristics. In contrast, socio-economic characteristics mainly determine deferred retirement. Therefore, the expectation that both, early and deferred retirement, are determined by the same factors with opposite sign cannot be confirmed. Accordingly, Hypotheses 2 – *Early and deferred retirement are determined by the same factors with opposite sign* – has to be rejected, although it seems reasonable at first sight. The results show that region, as a significant determinant has a positive odds ratio for both early and deferred retirement for individuals living in West Germany compared to individuals living in the east. Therefore, there are still regional differences concerning retirement age. Official data of the German Pension Insurance confirm this finding in

[159] See Appendix A.1.

[160] Each group of the dependent variables should have at least 25 cases (See Backhaus, 2011, p.480). The entire sample should contain at least 100 cases to achieve sufficient accuracy (See Urban, 1993, p.13).

case of early retirement. So, the average retirement age of old-age pension in 2008 for West Germany was 63.3, whereas for East Germany it was one year lower with 62.3.[161] Gender also affects early retirement. Former low employment rates of women combined with a special type of pension for women might be the main reason behind this. Due to the current ongoing positive trend in the labor market participation of women and the abolishment of this special pension type, the significance of gender in this context is supposed to decrease in future.

The level of education is relevant for early retirement. However, it is not a monotonic relationship. Individuals with a low level of education have the lowest probability to retire early, followed by individuals with a high education level. Middle qualified individuals have the highest probability to retire early. A simple interpretation might be the fact, that individuals with lower education are not able to accept deductions in their pension that come along with an early retirement. During their career their income was rather low, leading to a small amount of earning points with a low pension amount. Higher educated persons can afford a cut in their pension in favor of leisure. Why is this not a monotonic relationship? Worse job prospects of middle educated individuals compared to higher educated individuals might be a reason for this. Further, I suppose household income as another cause. The decision about when to retire depends not only on the individual pension amount but on the income of the household as a whole. This assumption may also be responsible for the independency of deferred retirement and the education level. Since the overall education level increases within the population, it is politically necessary to oppose strong incentives against early retirement.

Another variable that influences the retirement decision is the specific situation of the individual just before retirement. However, diverse aspects of the specific economic situation affect early and deferred retirement differently. Being already excluded from the labor market because of invalidity or unemployment increases the chances of early retirement. On the contrary, being a housewife/-man enhances the chances of deferred retirement. Several employment characteristics have an impact on early retirement, which point to a dominance of push factors when it comes to early retirement. In

[161] See Deutsche Rentenversicherung Bund (2011).

contrast, these push factors do not play a dominant role when it comes to deferred retirement.

Once an adequate pension is available, individuals make a trade-off by taking early retirement (by taking a loss in the pension amount) in order to have more leisure time. In contrast, deferred retirement is mainly determined by the pension of the individual and the pension of his or her partner. If the partner's pension is high, the individual seems to be motivated to defer his or her own retirement. Thus, in general Hypothesis 1 – *The retirement decision is determined by push factors, as well as by the social, educational and economic attributes of the individual* – can be confirmed.

A closer examination of the interdependence between the health status and an employment as retiree has been conducted. The common statement that an employment at higher ages is significantly depending on a good health status, seems only to be true in part. In general, the health status, which is measured by self-assessment of the respondents as well as the number of current physical diseases, of employed retirees is better on average. More precisely, the average results are better and the standard deviation is lower, therefore the group is more homogenous. However, the differences to the unemployed retirees are moderate. Further, in both groups, persons with above-average as well as below-average health status exist. Differentiating the unemployed retirees according to their intention to take up an employment, leads to similar results in the health status. Thus, the willingness to work as retiree is not strictly correlated with a good health status, but depends on several other determinants analyzed in this chapter. Conclusions about the direction of influence are hard to identify. Either a good health status promotes the intention to take up an employment as retiree, or being employed has positive effects on the health status of the retiree. Probably both are true and the size of the impact differs depending on the individual. It should be a major goal to promote health and physical functioning of every employee by arranging adequate working places. This should already be done in younger ages, though the requirements might change with age, or tasks and should be updated regularly. In doing so, the health status of the individual is minimal stressed and the companies benefit from longer working careers, as well as the elderly benefit from an ongoing participation in the labor force accompanied by positive effects on their physical ability and health.

The results of my analysis suggest that early retirement is mainly determined by employment and socio-demographic factors, whereas deferred retirement is dominated by factors related to income variables. This implies that push factors determine the decision to retire early and pull factors determine the decision to defer retirement. Hence, labor policy can be effective in diminishing early retirement. Recent developments of the labor market, which have been elaborated in section 3.3, seem in line with the aim to stabilize the retirement system. However, stemming early retirement is not enough. The duration of employment period has to be prolonged considerably. Regardless of the latest increase in retirement ages, a policy that is voluntary is more likely to be effective in extending the employment period. Further, these findings suggest that the policy of deductions for early retirement and bonuses for deferred retirement has a stronger impact on the decision to defer retirement than on the decision to retire earlier. This implication will be taken up in the next Chapter 5 and utilized to implement a modified rating system of earning points in the German pension scheme.

5 Age-specific Earning Points

Based on the findings of the previous chapters, my intention is to propose a modification of the existing German pension scheme in order to overcome the upcoming challenges of an aging society. I aim to do it in such a way that the individual's motivation to prolong his or her employment career will be stimulated. All reforms that directly affect the pension scheme, such as the increase of retirement ages, are rather unpopular and thus hard to implement by the politicians. Often, moderate amendments are enacted in order to mitigate the displeasure of voters. Instead of more cuts and restrictions in the pension scheme, why not embark on a reverse strategy? The major determinant of the individual retirement age is the statutory pension eligibility age. By setting such age limits, the government determines to a great extent the decision of the individual about when to retire. Usually, this implies at the same time an exit from the labor market. Thus, individuals are strongly geared towards the pension eligibility age. On the other hand, they demand greater flexibility. Ideally, age limits concerning retirement will be completely abolished. My suggestion works out this intention by providing strong incentives for keeping the elderly in employment. For this, age-specific earning points are implemented, which is an age-dependent modification of the existing earning points in the German pension scheme. Put simply, earning points are additionally weighted with increasing age.

5.1 Introduction

Tackling old-age poverty is one of the most demanding tasks of a welfare state. The German pension scheme, as a pay-as-you-go system, offers several pathways to retirement at different ages. Remarkable changes took place in 2007.[162] Compared to the previous regulations, the age for claiming a pension was raised by two years in regard to all options. Further, several alternative paths like partial retirement were omitted completely. Therefore, the number of possible pathways into retirement has decreased in general. Especially for women the pathways change, since the special

---

[162] Due to the RV-Altersgrenzenanpassungsgesetz (20.04.2007).

pension type for women no longer exists. Thus, the popular option for women to draw this pension starting already from the age of 60 belongs to the past. In consequence, the determinants of the retirement decision might also change. This analysis aims to provide a deeper understanding of the parameters influencing the retirement decision of the individual.

<table>
<tr><th></th><th>60</th><th>61</th><th>62</th><th>63</th><th>64</th><th>65</th><th>66</th><th>67</th><th>68</th><th>69</th></tr>
<tr><td>3 years of employment, 5 years of qualifying period</td><td colspan="7">pension due to reduced earning capacity</td><td colspan="3">old-age pension</td></tr>
<tr><td colspan="3">35 years of qualifying period</td><td colspan="8">old-age pension for severely handicapped persons</td></tr>
<tr><td colspan="4">35 years of qualifying period</td><td colspan="7">old-age pension for long-standing insured</td></tr>
<tr><td colspan="6">45 years of qualifying period</td><td colspan="5">old-age pension for especially long-standing insured</td></tr>
<tr><td colspan="8">5 years of qualifying period</td><td colspan="3">old-age pension</td></tr>
</table>

Source: own illustration based on Arnds and Bonin (2002).

Table 9: Pathways to retirement in Germany for individuals born in 1964 and later

Table 9 shows the possible pathways to retirement valid for all people born in 1964 and later (for individuals born before 1964 see Table 5 in chapter 4). While the pension eligibility age is 65 for individuals born before 1947 and will be in future 67 for individuals born in 1964 and later[163], there is, under certain circumstances, the possibility to retire earlier accepting a deduction in pension of 0.3% per month. In general, since over 50% of all pensions in 2010 were drawn with deductions[164], a strong tendency to retire as soon as possible can be observed. Further, the average number of months for which early pension was claimed is 36, which is a relatively long period.[165] Actuarial fairness seems to be violated. Moreover, early retirement seems even to be

[163] For individuals born between 1947 and 1964 an incremental increase of the statutory retirement age applies.

[164] See Deutsche Rentenversicherung Bund (2010).

[165] See Deutsche Rentenversicherung Bund (2010).

encouraged.[166] In chapter 4 I detected the fact of reaching the statutory retirement age as a major influence on the individual decision to retire. Obviously, the pension eligibility age strongly determines effective retirement age. Since the German population is aging, due to increasing life expectancies as well as decreasing fertility rates, the financing of a pay-as-you-go system is threatened. Increasing the pension eligibility age is one possible way to handle it. Nevertheless, an increase of two years bears no relation to the extent the population is ageing. Appropriate adjustments are politically hard to implement. A more flexible system, which takes into account differences in the retirement ages of individuals, is needed.[167] Simultaneously, the capable elderly should be encouraged to stay longer in employment and work more at higher ages.

Let me briefly recap the trends on the labor market discussed in detail in chapter 3.3. Afterwards, I will give a brief literature overview that is relevant for the topic of this study. The employment rate of persons aged 55+ is increasing constantly. The share of people over 50 among employees subjected to compulsory social security contributions increased from 17.9% in 1990 to over 22.7% in 2006 and 26.2% in 2010.[168] The underlying causes were on the one hand the aging of the high fertility age-groups as well as the rising employment rate of females in general. A longer stay in employment, i.e., a deferment of retirement also matters for this development. These positive conditions can be used to provide incentives for the elderly to continue work at higher ages and to postpone their retirement.

Kingston (2000) uses the Merton Model to calculate the efficient timing of retirement and enriches the familiar result that one should retire at the time when the disutility of work equals the marginal utility of another year's wage by the fact that one's exposure to risky assets should not increase dramatically at the point of retirement.

Himmelreicher and Stuchlik (2008) describe the development of the amount of individual earning points of new retirees between 1993 and 2007. Except for West

[166] See Breyer and Hupfeld (2009a).

[167] See Diamond (2005). He also states that the timing of drawing one's pension benefits and stopping work may be different for the profession of a worker.

[168] See Brussig (2011b).

German females, the margin of pensions enlarged. At the same time the median of earning points decreased by 6% during this period. Continuous employment is crucial for a high number of earning points. As Riedmüller and Willert (2008) show, even a relatively short unemployment phase of one to three years lead to financial losses of about 10% in the pension amount.[169]

Recent changes in employees' career histories are analyzed in a research project by the Hans Böckler Stiftung.[170] The German public pension system relies heavily on a long contribution period. Discontinuity, late entry into, or early exit from the labor market, all have a negative impact on individual pension amounts. The data shows a higher number of months being unemployed as well as longer education periods leading to a later entry into the workforce by younger cohorts, which, for that reason, have to expect lower pensions.

In a quantitative analysis Fehr et al. (2010) show that the current pension scheme in Germany is not able to stabilize the contribution rates in the long run. Therefore, old-age poverty rates will increase over the next years. Further, an increase in the statutory retirement age by two years will lead to an increase in the effective retirement age by about one year. Lastly, the rising actuarial adjustment of benefits may also lead to a noticeable increase of the effective retirement age.

Linking the pension receipt to a specific age is common, but age-dependent incentives are rare. One possibility is to differentiate the tax rate of pension payment or contributions. Age-dependent taxation through the retirement formula was first analyzed by Wredel (1999) and then extended by Fenge et al. (2002) and Kifmann (2008). It is shown that the optimal structure of age-dependent taxation can be characterized by a generalized Ramsey formula. Furthermore, the optimal retirement benefit formula is derived in the presence of a general tax system.[171] Another, more direct way of implementing age-dependent incentives is the implementation of age-

169 See Riedmüller and Willert (2008), p. 22, Table 2.

170 See Trischler und Kingstler (2011).

171 Other literature of age-dependent taxation without a link to the retirement benefit formula include Erosa and Gervais (2002), Fennell and Starck (2005), Lozachmeur (2006), and Blomquist and Micheletto (2008).

specific pension entitlements. For instance, Spain's earnings-related, public pension scheme provides higher accrual rates at younger ages.[172] However, the motivation to work longer at higher ages is affected thereby in a negative way. Finland is the only country I am aware of that implemented age-dependent accrual rates in 2005 to encourage longer working careers.[173] Several studies have confirmed the success of this reform. On the one hand Kannisto (2012) proves that the expected effective retirement age increased by approximately 1.5 years from the level prior to the pension reform and was 60.5 years in 2011. Moreover, Tenhunen (2010) shows that, the probability of continuing to work from 65 to 66 increased more than four times from 2003 to 2006.

This study contributes to the modification of pension schemes by implementing adequate incentives to encourage employment at higher ages and disburden the social security system at the same time. So far, my approach of age-specific earning points is the first to implement stronger age-dependent incentives to the German pension scheme. At best a statutory pension eligibility age is no longer needed.[174]

The structure of this chapter is as follows. Section 5.2 introduces the model and is followed by the analysis in Section 5.3. The results are discussed in Section 5.4. Finally, Section 5.5 concludes.

5.2 The model

I model the retirement decision as a Markov Decision Process (MDP). At each state the individual decides on an action, which maximizes the outcome of the resulting following states. The map between an action and a state is called strategy π. The set of all strategies is Π.

[172] After 15 years of contributions, the pension benefit is 50% of the earnings base. During the following ten years, for each year an extra 3% is accrued, followed by 2% per year thereafter. After 35 years of contributions the maximum accrual of 100% is reached (see OECD (2011), p. 310).

[173] At ages 18-52 the accrual rate is 1.5% of pensionable earnings, at ages 53-62 it is 1.9% and at ages 63-67 it is 4.5% (see OECD (2011), p. 224).

[174] If necessary the condition of reaching a certain amount of pension entitlement has first to be fulfilled in order to retire.

Formally, a MDP consists of the following tuple

$$(S, s_0, A, P_{sa}, \lambda, R)$$

with S being the set of all states, s_0 the starting state, A the set of all actions, $P_{sa}: S \rightarrow [0,1]$ the transitions probabilities, λ a discount factor and $R: S \rightarrow R$ the value function.

The valuation of a strategy $\pi \in \Pi$ results from the utility function $U: \Pi \rightarrow R$, which is defined by

$$U(\pi) = E\left[\sum_{t=0}^{\infty} \lambda^t \cdot R(s_t)|\pi\right]$$

Here, s_t are the states reached by the choice of actions of strategy π at time t while starting at a certain state s_0. Therefore, the optimal strategy π^* with the highest utility is given by

$$\pi^* = \max_{\pi \in \Pi} U(\pi)$$

and can be calculated by backward induction.[175]

In doing so, I am able to calculate the optimal retirement age for each individual based on the maximum expected payoff over a given planning horizon. In this model the expected payoff is represented by the utility function $U(\pi)$ and depends on the strategy that is chosen. In this framework the individual has the option to choose between three strategies: employment, retirement or death. Death is not really a choice but is determined by the survival probability for a certain age. Official data from the Federal Statistical Office is taken for this purpose. The payoff for the choice to stay in employment equals the net income of the individual. Likewise, the payoff of the choice to retire equals the net pension of the individual. Details about the exact calculation of both payoffs are given in the next section.

In the next step, I program my own java application based on the model I explained so far and use the payoffs as inputs. As output I get for each year within the planning

[175] See Rust (1994).

horizon for each possible choice of the individual the expected payoffs and the optimal strategy. This information can be used to identify the optimal age of the individual for switching his or her strategy of continuing employment into retirement.

Within the German pension system earning points play a key role. Insurants gather earning points during their career. In most cases the earning points come from employment, i.e., the contributions which are paid from it. But also for other states like education, parenting etc. earning points are given. After retirement they define the monthly pension amount. In general the so-called "*Teilhabeäquivalenz*" holds. This means that the relative income position during the career should be maintained also during retirement for the same cohort. In particular, if a person earns twice as much as another person born in the same year and thus pays twice as much contributions during the career, the pension should be also twice as high if both retire at the same time.[176]

A simple description of the current German pension formula is as follows:

$$monthly\ pension = \\ pension\ type\ factor * sum\ of\ earning\ points * current\ pension\ value * \\ pension\ access\ factor$$

The *current pension value* expresses the pension amount corresponding to an earning point and is regularly adjusted by the government. However, the *pension type factor* distinguishes between the several different types of pensions like old-age pension (= 1), invalidity pension (= 1), orphan's pension (= 0.2) and others. The *pension access factor* adjusts for deductions or bonuses in case of an early or a deferred retirement. *Sum of earning points* is the sum of all earning points achieved during the career and is computed by:

$$earning\ points = \frac{individual\ income\ liable\ for\ contribution}{average\ income\ of\ all\ employees}$$

Therefore, if the individual annual income equals the average annual income of all employees, the person gains exactly one earning point. If the annual income is higher,

[176] See Breyer and Hupfeld (2009b).

the value is bigger than one. If the annual income is lower, it is smaller than one. Obviously, the latter leads to a smaller pension amount in total.

5.3 Analysis

I use the scientific user file SUF-VVL 2007 from the FDZ[177], which contains completed insurant histories from 2007. The original data set consists of 34,437 cases with 142 variables, i.e., for each insurant the history starts in January of the year in which he reaches the age of 14 and continues over 624 months. I exclude all cases where the pension was calculated manually (#460), all kinds of pensions due to reduced earning capacities and all time-pensions (#3,468), all cases in which pension and income occurs simultaneously (#529) as well as all cases without at least one month of employment. Finally, 19,190 cases are left for further analysis. I match two data sets: MEGPT – the earning points for month x due to the social employment situation, and SES – the social employment situation for month x. In doing so, I am able to identify for each case the number of earning points achieved for month x including the information on what situation these points where given for.

In the next step I run a Two-Step cluster analysis[178] to get typical life histories of the insured persons. After clustering the number of months of the 13 different social employment situations for each case, I identify nine clusters, each representing a different typical career path. By performing an additional discriminant analysis, a good outcome of the clustering can be confirmed. Further, when my clustering is compared to the clustering results of Dlugosz[179], who used the same data set for a clustering procedure for discrete-time and discrete-valued life course trajectories that does not depend on a dissimilarity measure but on dispersions, both clustering outcomes match consistently. Thus, based on this clustering nine groups with typical life trajectories are identified. Basic characteristics of these nine cluster are summarized in Table 10 and Table 11.

---

[177] FDZ-Biografiedatensatz für die Biografiedaten zu Vollendeten Versichertenleben (VVL) 2007.

[178] For details of the Two-Step cluster analysis procedure see IBM_SPSS (2010b). The algorithms are explained in IBM_SPSS (2010a).

[179] See Duglosz (2011).

Descriptive statistics

Attributes	
Total number of cases	19,190
Gender	
male	12,007
female	7,183
Pension type	
old-age pension	9,758
old-age pension for women	6,648
old-age pension for long-standing insured	2,784
Married	14,825
Retirement age	
mean	63.49
minimum	60
maximum	65
Sum of Personal Earning Points[180]	
mean	28.18
minimum	0.9
maximum	74
Total number of months pre-drawing the pension	
mean	16.88
minimum	0
maximum	60
Total number of months postponing the pension	
mean	0.01

[180] Personal Earning Points include already deductions and bonuses from early or deferred retirement.

minimum	0
maximum	11
Years of employment	
mean	25.62
minimum	0.08
maximum	51.17

Table 10: Descriptive statistics of the data set

Figures 25 and 26 visualize the differences in career paths between the different clusters. In every cluster each career path begins with an education period (see pink color gradients in Figure 26). However, Cluster 1 and Cluster 7 show only a few pink areas, which might suggest a low education level. In contrast, long periods of education can be found in Cluster 8 and to some extent also in Cluster 5. Hence, these cluster are supposed to achieve a high level of education, often including academic studies. Female-dominated clusters have long periods of parenting (see yellow color gradients in Figure 26). Additionally, women have the option for a special pension type including early retirement at the age of 60. This leads to small amounts of personal earning points (see Table 11) because of deductions and the missed potential time to gather additional earning points. The pure male cluster achieves the highest amount of average personal earning points due to a long and continuous employment phase. Consequently, periods of parenting, unemployment, domestic care and even education lower the total employment time and therefore the amount of personal earning points. Clusters 6 to 8 show a relatively high number of earning points due to continuous employment (see red color gradients in Figure 26). Discrepancies in the amount of earning points between these clusters can be explained by differences in the income level and the level of education. Cluster 5, containing mainly self-employed individuals, has to be considered separately in this analysis, since the compulsory pension insurance expires with the beginning of self-employment. Clusters 1 to 4 achieve only a rather low amount of earning points. Compared with the top four clusters, the differences in the sum of earning points vary between -29%[181] and -76%[182]. To sum up, the cluster can be

[181] Cluster 8 compared to Cluster 2.

categorized as follows: cluster 1 to cluster 4 achieve rather low amounts of earning points and have discontinuous employment biographies in general; cluster 5 is a special case due to dropping out of the public pension insurance at the time of becoming self-employed; cluster 6 to cluster 8 achieve rather high earning points and have generally constant employment biographies. Taking another look at Figure 26, these differences can be easily detected. The first four clusters show white gaps during the career paths, which means that no activities relevant to earning points where done by the insurant. Moreover, there are few red paths of employment illustrated. In contrast, the last four clusters show almost no gaps during the career paths but a high number of long red paths of employment instead. What is the cause of such differences in earning points?

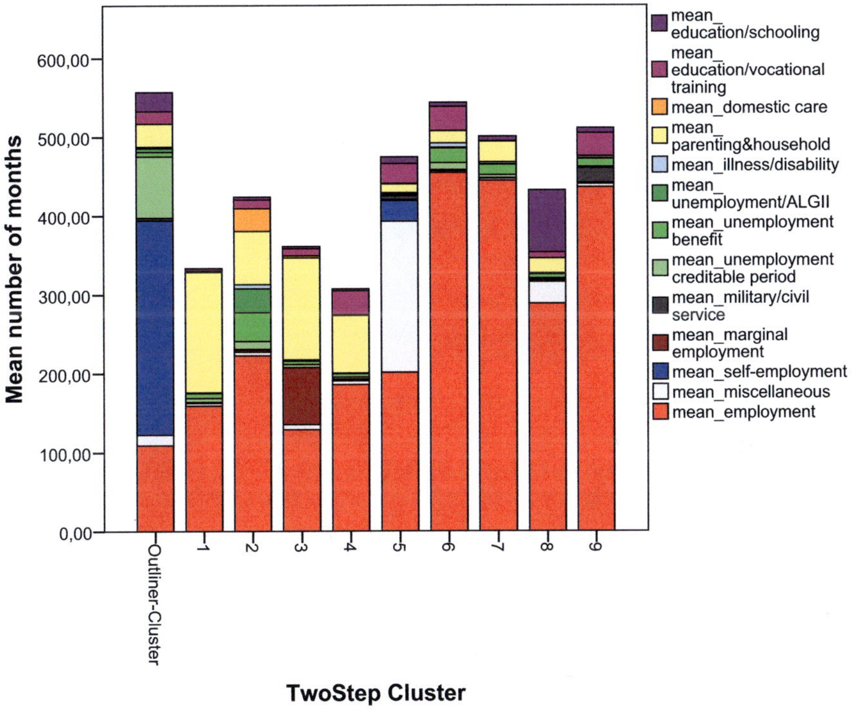

Source: own calculations.

Figure 25: Histogram of social employment situation trajectories of the cluster

Cluster 2 achieves almost 21 earning points, which is the highest value within the group of the four worst clusters. This cluster shows a middle level of education and periods of parenting. Further, some periods of employment are also given. Even though this is

---

[182] Cluster 9 compared to Cluster 3.

mostly part-time employment, it leads to relevant payment of contributions. The significant characteristics of this cluster are periods of domestic care at the end of the career path (see orange color gradients in Figure 26). Although domestic care is also credited with earning points, these periods would be credited much more with employment. Cluster 4 achieves almost 15 earning points, which is the second best within the group of the four worst clusters. In this cluster the education period is followed by a period of employment. The latter period is then interrupted by a period of parenting. A re-entry into the labor market followed only in some cases. Consequently, almost no relevant amounts of earning points were gathered during the second half of the career leading to a small amount of earning points at the end of the career. Cluster 1 achieves almost 13 earning points. This cluster contains mainly females and provides only a low education level. Besides periods of parenting, some employment periods are given, but they are based on minor employment coming along with low income. For this reason the total sum of earning points is low. The lowest sum of earning points is achieved by Cluster 3 with almost eleven earning points. Only rare periods of employment are the determining factor for the lowest amount in earning points.

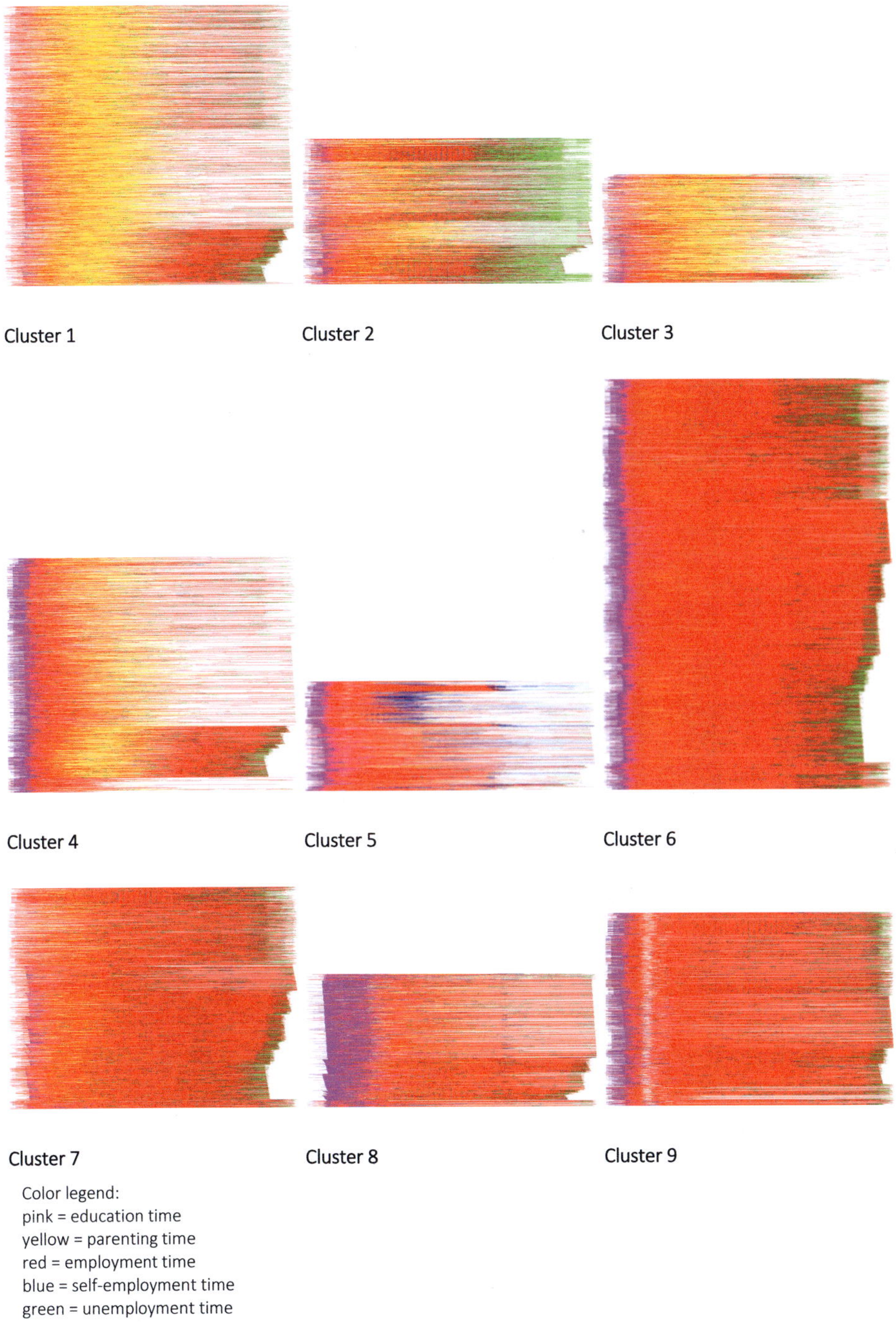

Figure 26: Colored career paths of the nine cluster

Cluster	**1**	**2**	**3**	**4**	**5**	**6**	**7**	**8**	**9**
Size	15.3%	7.9%	5.9%	12.8%	5.9%	22.4%	12.0%	7,2%	10,5%
Female	**99.7%**	76.3%	**94.7%**	67.0%	27.0%	59.2%	78.4%	40.0%	**0.0%**
Average number years of employment	13.27	18.55	10.75	15.50	16.77	**37.90**	**37.07**	16.77	**36.37**
Average number of months with deductions	11.08	**23.44**	9.39	11.59	8.04	**27.48**	**26.46**	8.37	8.35
Average personal earning points	13.72	21.26	11.47	15.25	26.64	**43.83**	36.91	36.66	**47.19**
Average earning points from employment	9.02	13.49	7.12	11.53	16.94	**38.26**	32.57	32.83	**42.44**
Social employment situation trajectory	Parenting, fractional employment	Education, parenting, fractional employment, unemployment, domestic care	Education, parenting, fractional and marginal employment	Education, employment, parenting	Higher education, employment, self-employment	Education, employment, fractional unemployment	Employment	Higher education, employment	Education, military/civil service, employment

Table 11: Cluster characteristics

Data Preparation

I calculate for each cluster the average monthly gross earnings on the basis of the average earning points from employment.[183] For the corresponding net earnings the average annual non-wage labor costs are subtracted. Furthermore, all values are inflation-adjusted (base year 2005). Since most individuals have the possibility to retire several years before the statutory retirement age of 65 and even 60 for women, the data shows a strong decline in earning points from employment between ages 60 and 65 resulting in low average salaries during these years. For this reason I smooth this decline by spline interpolation[184] of the ages 60 – 65 based on the data for ages 57 – 59 and 66 (the value for age 66 equals the average values of ages 60-65). From age 70 I assume a constant extrapolation. Figure 27 shows the developing of the fitted curves of average annual earning points from employment per cluster.

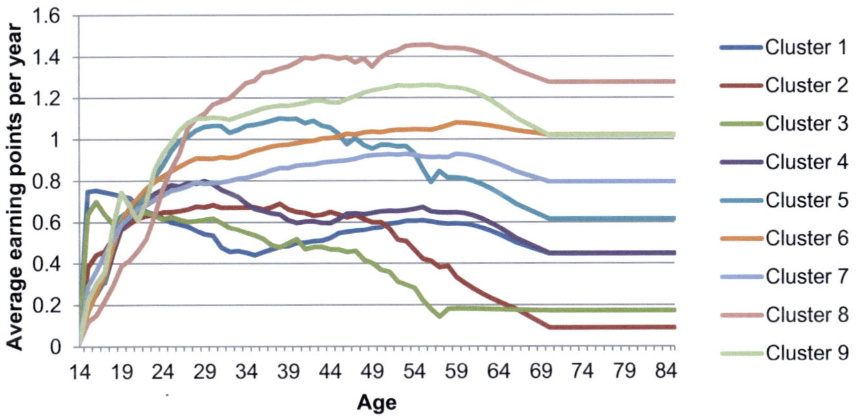

Source: own calculations.

Figure 27: Distribution of earning points

Likewise, I determine for each cluster the monthly net pension amount for different retirement ages by the average sum of personal earning points multiplied with the current pension value. Further, I adjust it by additional deductions and bonuses depending on the hypothetical retirement age as well as by the average increase or decrease of earning points from employment for additional or missed working years.

---

[183] I exclude zero values in order to avoid underestimation of the average salary.

[184] Cubic splines were used for interpolation.

The net pension amount is corrected by contributions to health and long-term care insurance and inflation-adjusted (base year 2005). This allows a direct comparison of net earnings and net pension amounts.

Modification of earning points

I model three scenarios summarized in Table 12, which differ in the level of increase (positive progressive, linear and negative progressive) of weights at a base of 6% increase per year.[185]

Scenario	expo	linear	ln
Increase of EP	positive progressive	linear	negative progressive
Formula	$EP * 1.06^t$	$EP + (1 + (t * 0.06))$	$EP * 1.06 * \ln(t)$

Table 12: Modification scenarios

Starting at three different ages, 50, 55 and 60, I calculate the impact of increases in the pension amount in the presence of age-specific earning points. I use the pension value of 2007 for West Germany, which was 26.13€, since this was the valid value for one earning point at the time of retirement of the individuals. The current pension value is higher and therefore the increments are higher today. Nevertheless, the relations have not changed because the earning points remain the basis of the pension amount calculation over the whole subscription period of the insurant. Table 13 shows the differences in increments conditional on the period during which the modified earning points are valid. Obviously, the longer this period is for example, if it starts already at the age of 55 and the individual works until the age of 75 the higher the increment is. On the one hand the gain must be large enough to fulfill the purpose as a strong incentive. At the same time it should not be too large to ensure financial efficiency of the pension insurance. I choose expo55, expo60, linear55 and ln60 for further analysis because the values satisfy both requirements and all are within a moderate range.

---

185 Currently the bonus for delaying the pension claim is 6% per year. Queisser and Whitehouse (2006) support the actuarial neutrality of such an increment in pension. However, some of the literature points out the increment in pension as rather too low for encouraging individuals to retire later (e.g. Werding (2007), Clemens (2004) and Gasche (2012a)).

Starting at the age of 55, when all individuals at the latest start giving thought to their retirement, the calculation is run over a planning horizon of 30 years. I choose a planning horizon of 30 years because it is in line with the average life expectancy of the cohort of the data set used for this analysis. Thus, the period is realistic for the individuals and biases in optimal ages are minimized.

	Working until 65	Working until 70	Working until 75
Expo50	182.07€	348.45€	590.18€
Expo55	81.10€	184.32€	343.39€
Expo60	19.54€	73.68€	170.98€
Expo65	-	17.47€	68.61€
Linear50	149.95€	247.95€	365.72€
Linear55	67.53€	138.25€	230.41€
Linear60	18.04€	61.47€	128.03€
Linear65	-	16.14€	57.10€
Ln50	324.62€	511.80€	709.92€
Ln55	143.92€	299.37€	475.20€
Ln60	22.26€	129.71€	275.85€
Ln65	-	19.88€	121.19€

Table 13: Increments in the pension amount resulting from modified earning points

5.4 Results

Before starting the evaluation of the modified and interpolated values, I run the modification with the pure data to check if the effective retirement ages of the cluster would also be calculated by my model. By comparing the observed retirement age in the data with the optimal age of retirement predicted by my model some divergences appear and are shown in Table 14. For detailed information about the distribution of the observed retirement age a boxplot diagram in Figure 28 is shown. For most clusters the optimal retirement age is much higher than the observed retirement age (with the highest value of 74). Three clusters (Cluster 2, 3 and 5) have an optimal retirement age of 60, which is the lowest possible age to draw the pension according to the old regulations (as shown in table 5). Cluster 5 contains individuals who became self-employed during their employment career and therefore dropped out of the statutory pension insurance automatically. Individuals in cluster 2 are forced into retirement due to domestic care and periods of unemployment. The cluster with the lowest amount of personal earning points is cluster 3, containing mostly females doing parenting and having some marginal employment, leading to poor chances on the labor market. Therefore, for these three clusters there exist some relevant reasons that explain the deviations from the optimal retirement ages.

Cluster	Average retirement age observed in the data	Optimal retirement age calculated by the model[186]	Relevant determinants by significant odd ratios[187]
1	64	65	-
2	63	60	*High pension of husband* (0.307)
3	64	60	*High pension of husband* (0.307)
4	64	66	*Female* (4.757)
5	64	60	*Small own pension* (4.586)
6	63	71	*Unemployment* (0.177)
7	63	74	*Female* (4.757)
8	64	70	*(High valuation of leisure)*
9	64	70	*(High valuation of leisure)*

Table 14: Retirement ages characteristics

[186] Calculation based on a starting age of 60 with a planning horizon of 25 years. The discount factor is set to 2%.

[187] The odd ratios are taken from my analysis in chapter 4.

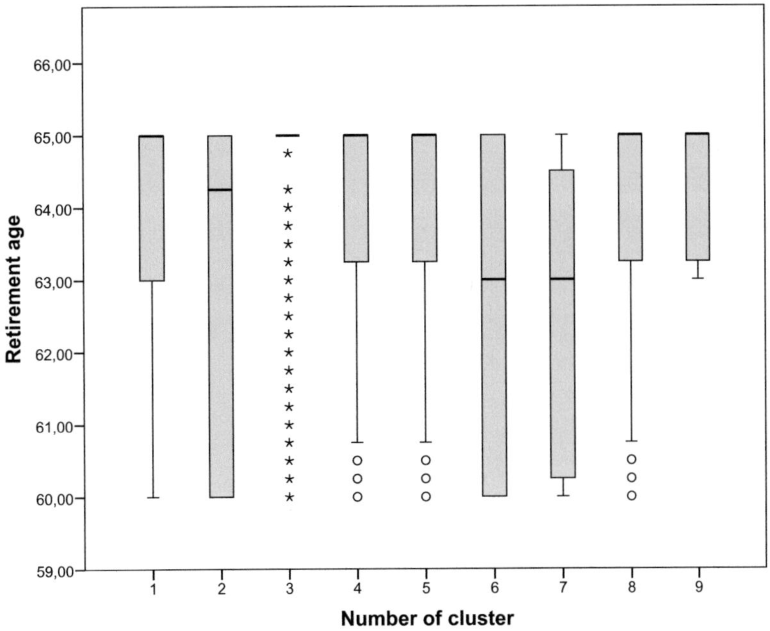

Source: own calculations.

Notes: * = extreme value (the gap between box height and the value is greater than 3 times)

° = outlier (the gap between value and the box height is between 1.5 times and 3 times)

Figure 28: Boxplot of observed retirement ages

The data shows that the age gap between the observed and the optimal retirement age is positive as well as negative. I explain this deviation using the results of our previous chapter, in which I determined odd ratios for early retirement as well as for deferred retirement. Deferring retirement is primarily driven by intrinsic motivation like fun at work and ongoing social contact, whereas several employment and socio-demographic facts favor early retirement. Cluster 1 matched the retirement age almost exactly and needs no further explanation. Cluster 2 and 3 (mostly females) are both underestimated because of the missing financial information of the husband in the data. These persons should optimally retire even earlier, but are somehow financially secured through a high pension of their partner and therefore they defer their own retirement in favor of a higher bonus. Cluster 5, however, is mostly male. Here the individuals are forced to defer their retirement because the amount of personal earning points is very low. Thus, a sufficient pension amount cannot be drawn at the optimal retirement age. The remaining clusters are all overestimated. Cluster 4 and 7 contain a lot of females who tend to retire early. Likewise do individuals who are unemployed just before their retirement like the ones in Cluster 6. For Cluster 8 and 9 I am not able to assign an odd ratio responsible for the underestimation. A high valuation of leisure could be the reason for retiring years before the optimal retirement age in order to enjoy more free time.

As we have seen, a generalization of individual preferences is not possible. To gain information about the whole population, average measures like clustering are necessary. This requires additional interpretation. For this reason, I conduct the study of determinants in chapter 4. The findings allow for a better evaluation of the model outcome.

In the next step, I run the calculation with the modified and interpolated values described in the previous section. The java application calculates for each year the expected value of future income depending on the decision whether to stay in employment or to retire. As outcome I get the optimal strategy including the expected payoff for each year within the planning horizon. The resulting optimal retirement ages for each cluster and alternative weighting are summarized in Table 15.

Cluster	Original data	Expo55	Expo60	Linear55	Ln60
1	64	69	73	69	71
2	63	60	61	60	61
3	64	63	64	63	64
4	64	68	71	68	70
5	64	66	68	67	68
6	63	68	69	68	68
7	63	68	68	68	68
8	64	71	74	72	72
9	64	68	68	68	68
Average	*63.67*	*66.78*	*68.44*	*67*	*67.78*

Table 15: Optimal retirement ages

Cluster 1 – 4 predominantly include individuals with short employment periods and a low amount of earning points over time (compare the four lower curves in Figure 23). Cluster 5 has to be considered separately since it mostly consists of individuals becoming self-employed during their careers and therefore dropping out of the compulsory participation. However, Cluster 6 – 9 contain individuals with nearly full working careers and a relatively high amount of earning points in total (compare the four highest curves in Figure 27).

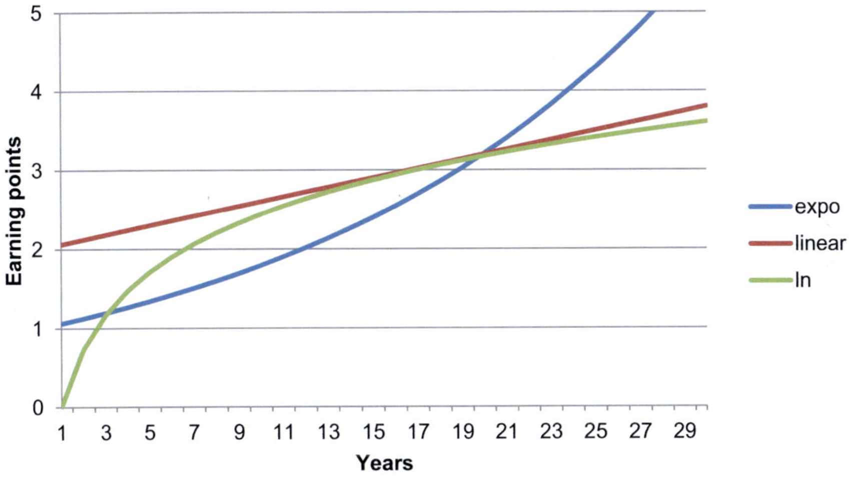

Source: own calculations.

Figure 29: Comparison of increments

Figure 29 shows the rising paths of the three slopes (exponential, linear and logarithmic) from a base of one earning point per year. In the linear case the slope is uniformly distributed, regardless of the number of additional working years, by contrast, in the exponential case the slope rises with a stronger intense over time. In the logarithmic case the slope declines over time. Until the 16th year of employment, the linear increase weights the earning points most heavily. After the 3rd year, the logarithmic increase exceeds the exponential one. All the time the extent of the logarithmic increase is smaller than that of the linear increase. From the 20th year of employment the exponential increase is stronger than the linear one. Depending on the starting age at which the earning points are modified (in my study it is 55 and 60 respectively) working 20 years onwards is rather unlikely. Here, the relevant period lies between 10 and 15 years. Table 16 shows the average final pension amounts of the original data as well as of the chosen modifications depending on the optimal retirement ages listed in Table 15. Individuals belonging to cluster 1 retire optimally between 69 and 73 and gain a surplus of about 46% – 49% in pension amount. As this cluster contains 99.7% female persons, this improvement is desirable since women face a greater risk of poverty.[188] Cluster 2 gets a shortfall in pension of about 16%. However, the optimal retirement ages are 60 or 61 and much lower than they were originally. Individuals of this cluster face a high probability of being unemployed and/or giving domestic care. Therefore, the incentives are not effective and affected individuals are forced to retire as soon as possible. Cluster 3 retires optimally almost at the same age as in reality, resulting in almost no change in pension or a discount of at most 9.26%. Members of the mixed cluster 4 work optimally until an age of 68 – 71 and get a surplus between 42% and 45%. Self-employed individuals gathered in cluster 5 gain between 24% and 33%, whereas their optimal retirement ages rise to 68. The results for cluster 6 and 7 are very similar. In all modifications the optimal retirement age is 68, resulting in a surplus of pension between 24% and 31%. Members of these clusters have the steadiest employment histories and a relatively high amount of earning points at the end of their career. Cluster 8 gains the highest surplus of about 50% in all four modifications. However, the optimal retirement age takes also the highest value of all outcomes and ranges between 71 and 74. This cluster consists of more highly educated individuals with relatively high income and therefore leads to a late retirement age as a rational strategy of the individuals. All-male members of cluster 9, who did military or civil service, work optimally until an age of 68 in all modifications and gain a surplus between 18% and 27%.

[188] See Deutsche Rentenversicherung Bund (2010).

Cluster	Original data	Expo55	Expo60	Linear55	Ln60
1	341.90€	663.35€ +48.46%	664.72€ +48.56%	635.39€ +46.19%	649€ +47.32%
2	510.32€	438.01€ -16.51%	439.61€ -16.09%	437.45€ -16.66%	439.61€ -16.09%
3	286.21€	285.81€ -0.14%	261.96€ -9.26%	284.51€ -0.6%	273.06€ -4.82%
4	378.39€	692.84€ +45.39%	657.15€ +42.42%	669.49€ +43.48%	667.48€ +43.31%
5	680.52€	952.52€ +28.56%	900.17€ +24.4%	1,016.97€ +33.08%	933.39€ +27.09%
6	1069.61€	1,543.56€ +30.70%	1,467.84€ +27.13%	1,499.5€ +28.67%	1,444.4€ +25.95%
7	895.52€	1,298.08€ +31.01%	1,173.68€ +23.7%	1,261.73€ +29.02%	1,214.59€ +26.27%
8	933.11€	1,887.48€ +50.56%	1,828.81€ +48.98%	1,867.23€ +50.03%	1,800.47€ +48.17%
9	1205.35€	1,659.30€ +27.36%	1,478.14€ +18.45%	1,611.38€ +25.2%	1,531.51€ +21.3%
Average	*700.10€*	*1,046.77€ +27.27%*	*985.79 € +23.15%*	*1,031.52€ +26.49%*	*994.83€ +24.28%*

Table 16: Final pensions

The results indicate a purposive effect of age specific earning points. The majority of individuals (86.2% of the dataset) benefit in form of higher pensions with moderate extensions of their working life. Shortfalls in pension affect only cluster 2 and to a small extent also cluster 3.[189] These individuals belong to society groups with careers of mainly fractional and marginal employment, often combined with parenting and

[189] Both clusters represent merely 13.8% of cases.

domestic care. In these cases the incentive to stay longer in employment is rather inadequate and to this subgroup an alternative support should be given. Particularly individuals with low earning points due to lower wages in their working lives, who are gathered in cluster 1 and 4, gain the highest surplus in pension amounts. Thus, especially for individuals with lower incomes, threatening old-age poverty will be mitigated to some extent. Cluster 8, which represents individuals with higher education and continuous employment at higher wages, attains the highest surplus in pension amount at a price of a large extension of the working life. Working continuously up to an age of 70 and more seems maybe not to be practicable for the majority. However, in the case of an earlier exit from the labor force these individuals still gain an appropriate surplus. Accordingly, the net pension replacement rates increase in all the modifications. In comparison to other OECD members, the net pension replacement rates of the German pension scheme belong to the lower third of all OECD countries.[190] After implementing age-specific earning points Germany's position will improve to the highest third. Further, the current German pension scheme provides worse incentives for lower or middle earners to stay in work.[191] Although the level of pension wealth at age 60 is very low, the change in pension wealth from working age 60 – 65 is also the lowest in Germany among all OECD countries. Again, age-specific earning points are able to correct this drawback.

From the perspective of the insurance institution the financing of a new reform has to be sustainable. Whilst taking into account the life expectancy of 65-year old individuals in 2007, which is 20.31 years for women and 16.93 years for men, the expenses in form of pensions and the incomes in form of contributions are offset and listed in Table 16.[192] In comparison to the current pension scheme two modifications have a cost overrun of about 84,000€ and 8,000€ respectively. Further two modifications even gain a marginal surplus of about 211,000€ and 113,000€ respectively. The subsample of this analysis

[190] See OECD (2011), p. 125.

[191] See OECD (2011), p. 55ff.

[192] The average life expectancy of a cluster is weighted by the percentage of female or male members and their corresponding life expectancies.

reflects merely about 2.7% of the underlying retiring cohort.[193] The bottom row of Table 17 shows the enlarged values. The total expenses for old-age pensions in 2007 were 161,299,000€.[194] Accordingly, the cost overrun of the modifications amounts to 1.9% in the worst case (expo55) or to savings of 4.8% in the best case (expo60). These moderate effects do not threaten financial stability and, in fact, indicate a sustainable concept for old-age poverty reduction and supporting long-lasting working careers.

Cluster	Cost overrun Expo55	Cost overrun Expo60	Cost overrun Linear55	Cost overrun Ln60
1	27,970€	-13,157€	22,498€	4,778€
2	-7,697€	-10,770€	-7,862€	-10,770€
3	2,313€	-6,152€	1,968€	-3,336€
4	30,743€	-7,587€	26,205€	4,400€
5	30,364€	-9,546€	27,257€	-3,629€
6	-3,512€	-41,664€	-11,932€	-22,461€
7	1,747€	-22,983€	-5,479€	-14,850€
8	9,919€	-66,309€	-3,794€	-12,832€
9	-7,479€	-32,984€	-40,995€	-54,346€
Total	84,368€	-211,154€	7,867€	-113,047€
Expansion	3,124,726€	-7,820,501€	291,359€	-4,186,923€

Table 17: Cost overrun of the modified public pension scheme

5.5 Concluding remarks

Age-specific earning points are effective in two ways: on the one hand by stemming early retirement and fostering a higher effective retirement age to stabilize the financial feasibility of the public pension system. On the other hand they lower the risk of old-age

[193] See Deutsche Rentenversicherung Bund (2008). Since the subsample considers only old-age pensions, the corresponding total number of insurants drawing an old-age pension is 704,461.

[194] See Deutsche Rentenversicherung Bund (2010).

poverty deriving from low pension amounts. Both are accomplished by providing explicit incentives for working at higher ages. I choose four different modifications starting the weighting of earning points at 55 or 60. These modifications differ in their progression of weighting. The average retirement ages increase on average by 3 to 5 years. As a result, the average pension amounts of the retirees increase between 23% and 27% on average, especially clusters of individuals with discontinuous biographies gaining the highest surplus.

Compared to the recent concept of a *grant pension* ("Zuschussrente") presented by the Secretary of Labor, age-specific earning points overcome the main points of criticism. Gasche (2012b) demonstrates that the *grant pension*, which is intended to increase low pensions of individuals with a continuous employment history, involves substantial discrimination and negative incentives to work. Instead, he proposes a *bonus pension* ("Bonusrente"), which is eligible for individuals with less than 31 earning points in total. They get for each year above 15 years of contributions a fixed bonus of earning points, which is equal for all insurants. He shows that the distortions as well as the discrimination can be reduced. Nevertheless, the *bonus pension* still provides negative incentives to work.

By implementing age-specific earning points employment at higher ages is honored in a special way. The effective retirement age will increase automatically; so will the employment rate of the elderly. Furthermore, the risk of old-age poverty diminishes. These are all crucial aspects for a pension scheme to be effective and sustainable in the long run.

This study has several limitations. First, it takes into account only regular old-age pensions. Other forms of pensions, especially pensions due to limited earning capacity, are not considered. I assume the individuals to have the capacity to work, although the interpolation is at a rather low income level and might reflect part-time employment in the last years before retirement. At the same time I assume the labor market to be adaptable to the demographic developments. Certainly, specific structural changes are required to offer employment opportunities for the elderly.[195] It is not the aim of the study to analyze this. However, statistical data indicates an ongoing trend: the employment rate of persons aged 60 – 65 and 65 and higher has risen continuously over the last years.[196] In addition another weighting factor may be considered that accounts for arduous work. Chile's pension scheme already does so and decreases the statutory retirement age by 1 – 2 years for every 5 years of arduous work. In this model, instead of a fixed retirement age, an additional weighting factor may have the same effect by making it possible to reach a sufficient amount of earning points earlier in the career. Obviously, the risk of increasing claims for invalidity pensions exists.[197] Increasing the retirement age enlarges the group of insurants who might be eligible for such a pension. Since this scheme does not include a fixed retirement age but strong incentives to retire later, this is a rather involuntary effect and not a real avoidance strategy.

Extensions of this model are necessary to model a variety of external effects like the unemployment rate or the probability of illnesses or diseases and are left for future research. Setting adequate weights is crucial for the financial stability of the pension scheme. Additional research is needed to assess the appropriate ones. In this context, my modifications may be possible candidates. Overall the outcomes of the four modifications do not differ drastically. So, for a right choice more information about the insurant as well as the macroeconomic development has to be taken into account. In any case, differences in life expectancy could be corrected where appropriate. For example, distinctions in premiums of private insurance contracts due to gender are no longer conformable to law, even though life expectancy differs by gender. Here, redistributions are desirable and socially acceptable. This holds especially true for social insurances like public pensions. In contrast, differences in life expectancies because of different income levels should be corrected. It is politically desirable to improve the old-age provision of low earners. A positive correlation of income and life expectancy has

---

[195] For example abolish fixed retirement ages set by collective labor agreements, enable job rotation and/or reduce working hours.

[196] See Statistisches Bundesamt (2012e), p.144.

[197] See Bäcker (2012).

been proven by several studies.[198] For this reason a declining assignment of earning points by income is proposed by Breyer (2013). The same effects can be achieved using weighting factors, additionally including strong incentives to prolong employment.

Thus, my approach of age-specific earning points appears to be effective in stabilizing the public pension scheme by setting adequate incentives without increasing inequality.

[198] See e.g. Breyer and Hupfeld (2009c).

6 Conclusion and outlook

The intention of this thesis is to contribute to the research in the field of retirement. More precisely, it aims to fill observed gaps in the literature on delayed retirement and on the incentives for employment at higher ages. Since German society is aging, it is necessary to explore the needs, potentials and motives of the elderly. Pensions are one of the major topics in politics. Adjusting retirement ages, preventing old-age poverty, integrating the elderly into the labor market, supporting health care and many other aspects directly or indirectly influence the old-age provision and require political support and/or regulations. As mentioned before, I concentrate on the motives for a delay of retirement in order to deduce incentives for prolonged employment at higher ages. In doing so, I am able to modify the existing German public pension system in such a way that the statutory retirement age is no longer the main determinant for the retirement time of an individual. Instead, by implementing weighting factors to the retirement formula, a higher valuation of employment at higher ages takes place, which strongly motivates capable potential retirees to stay in the labor market.

Figure 30 visualizes the structure of this thesis. Starting with the motivation about the politically charged topic of the aging society, I identify gaps in recent literature in regard to contributing to the discussion about social challenges deriving from demographic changes. It becomes evident that various researches have been done in the field of early retirement. In contrast, delayed retirement has not been intensively elaborated so far. Further, no extensive discussion of employment beyond retirement age has taken place. Of course, such a topic is politically not popular, because retirement still equals the exit from the labor market. Obviously, every deferment of the statutory retirement ages and/or cut in pension displeases voters. On the one hand, the aging of society requires an appropriate modification of the pension system in order to handle the effects of demographic change. The main effects are: a growing number of retirees, longer pension payment periods because of continuously increasing life expectancies, and a decline in the number of contributors as a consequence of low birth rates. On the other hand, all these effects lead to a growing majority of the elderly in society, representing the target group of the politicians. This discrepancy hampers the government in its attempts to enforce relevant modifications in the pension scheme that might be unfavorable for the current society, but will be favorable for the future society in the long run.

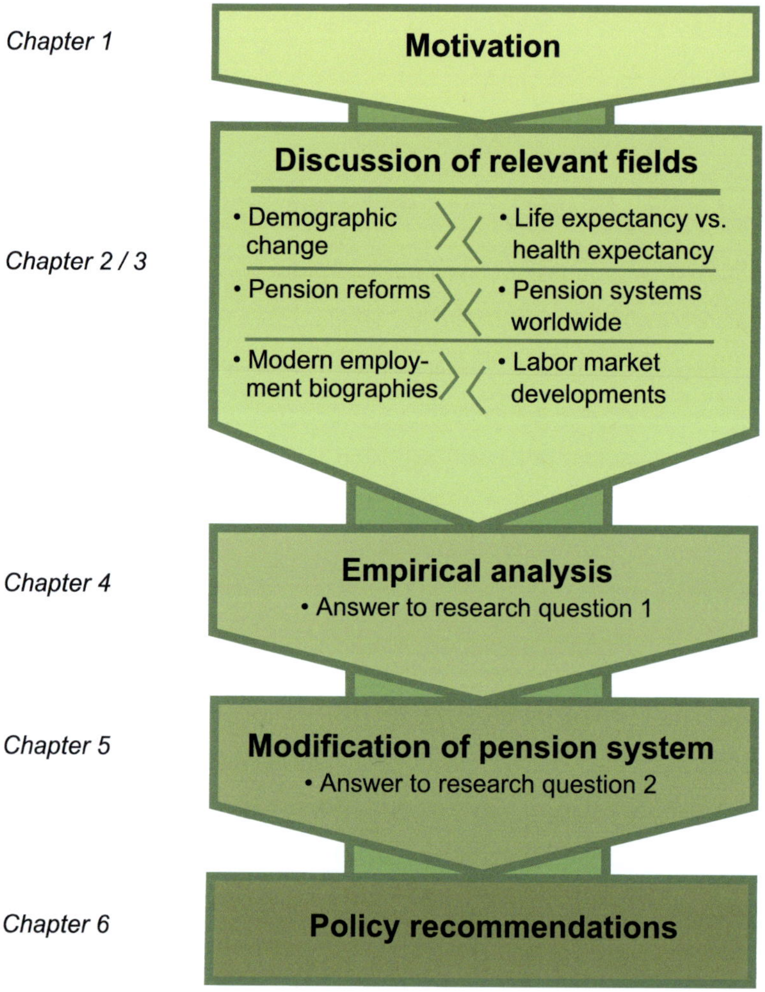

Figure 30: Structure of the thesis

Having this trade-off in mind, my intention is to avoid limitations that might affect retirees, elderly employees or any other group in society. Instead, I propose a modification that includes strong incentives for the elderly to continue employment at higher ages. This will not be perceived as discrimination in regard to the individual, but as an extra reward, motivating ongoing employment. Therefore, political resentment is minimized and the sustainability of the pension system ensured.

6.1 Conclusion

One of the relevant topics accompanying adaptions of the pension scheme is first of all demographic change. Starting with the baby boom in many industrialized countries around 1950, the share of the working age population increased over the following years, leading to an all-time high in the percentages of the elderly in the population today. Moreover, industrialization provides developments in social security, health care and education. All prolong the life time of the individuals. Since more than 100 years, the average life expectancy had increased at a nearly linear rate of about three months yearly. This is true for both genders.

At the same time, modern societies enable women to enter the labor market and start their own career equivalent to that of the men. Positively affecting gender equality, the new trends cause a decline in birth rates at the same time. Unfortunately, women often have to decide either in favor of having children or in favor of their own career. Coexistence is difficult to manage and the need for more support by the government and society is still unmet. Additionally, higher education shifts to higher ages the point of time of becoming pregnant. This means that the overall period of being able to give birth is shortened. In consequence, the average number of children per women is decreasing.

Increased life expectancy combined with ongoing low fertility rates causes the population to age and changes the demographic structure of the society. It concentrates no longer on the working population, but is shifting to higher ages, namely, the elderly. In principle, such a development does not have to be negative. In contrast, a longer life time should be in general an advantage for every human being. The crucial point is whether these extra years can be spent in good health or not.

So far, no consensus has been reached whether the theory of the expansion of morbidity or the theory of the compression of morbidity will prevail in the future. Literature provides evidence for both options. The first predicts just a longer period of suffering before death. The latter, instead, forecasts spending the extra years in good health and delaying the time of suffering and death into higher ages. The health status can be measured by medical check-ups and performance tests. However, the overall well-being determines, to a great extent, the self-reported health status of the individual. Thus, not only diagnoses, but the ability of the individual to cope with it, reflect the health status properly.

Changes in life and health expectancy in particular, should be reflected by reforms of the pension system. Germany was the first country worldwide that established a statutory public pension system in 1889. Until now, numerous reforms have been made. Most of them have been caused by the demographic change and aim to absorb the consequences, such as the most recent reform of raising the general statutory retirement age from 65 to 67, for example. Nevertheless, the linking of retirement ages with life expectancies is unbalanced and results in a lower raising of retirement ages than is necessary. Since 1995 many western European countries have tended to free themselves from the "Bismarck pension trap", in order to break the traditional role of the public pension scheme as the major income source of retirees. In Germany, the public pension is still the major income source of retirees. Despite government efforts to promote private pensions by tax reliefs and bonuses, the participation rate is only moderate. Moreover, the participation rate is particular low in low income households. This is counterproductive, inasmuch as especially these households should have an additional financial source for retirement to avoid old-age poverty.

Reforms that affect the retirees or the employees directly are unpopular and politicians avoid any publicity coming along with them. If at all, such reforms are moderated or hardly discussed before their implementation. An indirect implementation of reforms, for example on the labor market, would be a smarter method. Here, some ideas for a more flexible coexistence of earnings and pension have been proposed lately.[199] However, often disincentives arise and thus, these proposals do not provide a sustainable solution.

[199] The „Kombirente" was supposed to extend, simplify and flexibilize considerably the limit of additional income from employment, but it has not been implemented by the government during the last election period (see http://www.sueddeutsche.de/wirtschaft/hinzu-verdienst-durch-minijobs-ab-euro-ist-schluss-1.1641574 (11.07.2013)).

A worldwide comparison of pension schemes reveals similarities as well as differences between countries. Studies that evaluate the general performance of pension schemes often rank Germany in the midfield. The European trend of broadening the pension scheme into several pillars (i.e., public, occupational and private) and strengthening the share of funded pensions, changes the assets structure of private households. A higher share of individually funded pension plans means a detachment from the intergenerational contract, which is favorable regarding demographic changes. Nevertheless, also funded pension plans are linked via interest rates to economic performance, which depends on the working population and therefore on the demographic development. So, new risks, like financial crises, arise. As worldwide pension assets are growing, an adequate evaluation and control is necessary. The heterogeneity of global pension systems is still a hallmark (see Figure 14). However, a harmonization is taking place. Central and eastern Europe is catching up with the USA and Asia, although the differences in the share of funded pension assets are still high. The transition in Europe just started a couple of years ago. Therefore, it will still take some time.

The promotion of private pensions shifts to an increasing extent the old-age provision to the individual. In doing so, attention must be paid to deficiencies in individual decision making. Behavioral economics might provide good instruments to control the negative effects. Besides this, education has to close gaps in financial literacy among the population. Only by having full information is it possible to make the right decision on old-age provision.

Furthermore, the increasing participation rate of women on the labor market is one of the main achievements in gender equality and a surplus for the economy. Yet, other valuable services like parenting or domestic care are still predominantly offered by women. Modern forms of employment, such as part-time employment, allow for a combination of family and employment. Thus, part-time and other forms of atypical employment are becoming more popular, not only for women. The share of atypical employment is rising and is changing the employment biographies of the individuals. In general, more flexibility might be beneficial for the economy. For example, seasonal fluctuation can be absorbed by temporary employment, which might also be favorable for some employees. However, any discontinuity of employment as well as fewer working hours than full time directly lowers pension entitlements. At the time of the establishment of the German pension system, such modern career paths did not exist. So far, the valuation by earning points seems fair and reasonable. A modification is pending. Another subgroup of the modern labor market that is even completely excluded from the public pension insurance or any other compulsory pension scheme includes most self-employed individuals. In particular, the increasing share of solo self-employed means regulations are needed to ensure their old-age provision, as the solo self-employed often do not save at all for their retirement. Whether it is because of low income or because of unwillingness is of secondary importance. Either way, their pensions are not assured and might have to be paid in future by society if they claim social security.

Until now, public pensions are the major income source for German retirees. Occupational pensions only cover about every second employee. Indeed, companies make use of additional benefits in order to attract and maintain qualified staff members. Hence, occupational pensions, as a part of the employment contract, are becoming more and more the rule. Certainly, this option eludes most atypical employees. Likewise, less than every second person, who is eligible for a Riester pension, has one. The Riester pension, as a government-funded private pension, is supposed to close the pension gap deriving from cuts in public pensions. Again, lower income households show especially low participation rates. Thus, old-age poverty is a highly controversial topic. Even though there exists a means-tested basic protection for the needy, which can be claimed by retirees with an income below the subsistence level, it is becoming harder to achieve an earning-point position considerably above the subsistence level, due to cuts in the generosity of the public pension (see Figure 7). This fact challenges the motivation of the current public pension scheme.

One might argue that future retirees could rely on bequests considering that bequests of the recent decade have been so large like never before in Germany. During the post-war period it was possible to accumulate wealth that would be passed on to the next generation in the upcoming years. But these bequests are allocated unequally. Some few individuals will inherit large amounts, whereas the majority will inherit rather low amounts. Furthermore, often the wealth is passed on to individuals who are already well situated.[200] Thus, a complementing of pensions by bequests is generally not possible. The tendency is even supposed to worsen, since the life expectancy is increasing, and individuals will consume a larger share of their wealth. Healthcare costs will reduce the wealth as well. In sum, bequests will probably decrease in future and are not a reliable compensation for pensions for the majority of retirees.

Instead, it will be necessary to prolong one's own career and combine retirement with employment. So far, additional employment alongside a pension is rare. Yet, as the employment rate of the elderly rises continuously, an increase might be anticipated. The jobs that are performed the longest vary from executive or academic positions to farming or jobs in the service industry. But these cases are rather exceptions. Several studies show that the majority does not want to work after retirement. If at all, they consider working part time and with reduced working hours. When the motives for ongoing employment as a retiree are analyzed, staying fit is mentioned most often. On the other hand, major barriers to employment at higher ages are the lack of flexibility and poor health promotion. Both are currently not provided by the labor market. Hence, the general refusal of an employment at higher ages is comprehensible.

Nevertheless, there are possibilities to overcome this unwillingness. Age management measures are effective in promoting long-lasting employment. These measures can be categorized into one of the three main fields of action: qualification, health promotion and labor organization. The higher the number of measures that are offered in a company, the higher the working ability of the elderly is. Lifelong learning, various health services, ergonomic workplaces and flexible working time arrangements ensure the productivity and motivation of the older employees. Thus, employers benefit from the knowledge and routine of the older employees, and the employees benefit from the positive influence of employment on the physical and mental abilities.

I started my empirical analysis with the intention of exploring the group of retirees who defer their retirement and contrasting them to the group of retirees who retire as early as possible, even accepting deductions in the pension amount. Thus, in contrast to

---

[200] See Braun (2011).

other research so far, I am the first to consider the determinants of early and deferred retirement in a unified framework. Using a multiple logistic regression, I analyzed these determinants and contrasted them with regular retirement in order to prove my following two hypotheses:

Hypothesis 1: *The retirement decision is determined by push factors, as well as by the social, educational and economic attributes of the individual.*

Hypothesis 2: *Early and deferred retirement are determined by the same factors with opposite sign.*

Early retirement can best be explained by socio-demographic factors as well as employment characteristics, whereas deferred retirement is predominantly influenced by socio economic factors. Overall, hypothesis 1 can be proved. However, in contradiction to hypothesis 2, the lessons that can be drawn from the evidence on early retirement cannot contribute to an understanding of how to encourage individuals to work longer. Instead, stemming early retirement and promoting employment at higher ages have to be considered separately and require different political actions as well. The results of my empirical analysis suggest that early retirement does not depend on the income or accumulated wealth of the individual. Rather, it depends on a mixture of employment and socio-demographic characteristics. Reaching the pension eligibility age was the main reason for the termination of the last employment. Also operational reasons and poor health conditions lead to an exit from the labor market. Age management measures promoting the employability of the elderly can counteract these facts and foster ongoing employment.

Education is also a determinant for early retirements. Indeed, the relationship is not monotonic, but middle educated individuals work the shortest. It seems that current deductions do not deter them from retiring as early as possible. Trends like the increasing participation rate of women in the labor market have to be supported by providing child care opportunities. If this is done, some women might not decide against children in favor of a career, but will be able to do both. This leads to an increasing employment rate of women, which allows their productivity to promote economic growth, and raise their own pension entitlements.

The developments will significantly change the household structure in future, affecting the retirement decision and the income. While today most of the retirement households are still primarily financed by the pension of the husband or male partner, linked with a dependency of the wife or female partner, in future both will provide their own pension for retirement. This will be essential for accumulating a sufficient pension amount for the household, since the generosity of the public pension will decrease. This decrease is on purpose to share the burden of the aging population across the society.

In contrast to early retirement, deferred retirement mainly depends on the income of the individual's partner. If the income of the household as a whole is large enough, the individual has no need to claim his or her own pension as soon as possible, but has the opportunity to gain the bonuses for deferring his or her pension. Accordingly, being a housewife enhances the chances for deferred retirement. Since the potential income of the wife was not required to cover the costs of living of the household until retirement, it will not be crucial at the time of retirement and thereafter. Furthermore, working after retirement is rare. In general, the motivation for employment is not monetary but social, i.e., having fun and social contacts.

To sum up, labor policy is the key starting point to promote employment at higher ages. Age management measures are effective for this purpose and have to be promoted. Deductions for early retirement do not deter most of the retirees from retiring as early as possible. However, bonuses for deferring retirement appeal to well-situated individuals or households. Neither the first, nor the latter should be desired. Instead, early retirement should entail deductions that strongly discourage individuals from claiming the pension too soon. At the same time, bonuses should reward individuals, who prolong their employment (and not the role as a housewife) and pay additional contributions. This answers my first research question about the determinants and reasons concerning delayed retirement.

Next, the previous conclusions have been utilized to develop the modification of age-specific earning points within the current German public pension system. According to their own statements, individuals are very sensitive towards retirement age limits. Due to remarkable changes on the labor market, careers are becoming less durable. Instead, many employment biographies show different stages and discontinuities, involving a variety from unemployment and parental leave to gap years and sabbaticals. Employees seek for maximum flexibility and want to maintain it even after retirement. In particular, the transition into retirement should no longer be radical but fluent. This vision can only with difficulty be fulfilled by a public pension scheme that runs as a PAYGO system like the one in Germany. An aging society requires a long contribution period and an appropriate payback period as well. These periods should be consistent with the increasing life expectancies. Partial payments are not intended to be high enough to cover living costs. Additional employment might fill the financial gap but does not compensate the missing contributions in the long run.

According to recent studies and trends discussed in the thesis, an increase of average health expectancy can be assumed. Thus, a lengthening of the employment period into higher years can be justified, especially when taking into account longer education periods and diverse time-outs within the biography. Age-specific weighting points aim to encourage individuals to work at higher ages by rewarding their contributions to an increasing extent with age. In my model I propose four different modifications of age related weighting of earning points. The age-specific weighting starts either at 55 or 60. Further, the modifications differ in their progression of weighting. I cluster data from the German public pension insurance according to typical employment biographies and run a self-coded java application to check the modified pension scheme. The model is based on a Markov Decision Process that derives the optimal retirement age of an individual by maximizing expected future payoffs. Further, survival probabilities are included. Depending on the choice of weighting, the average retirement ages go up by 3 to 5 years. At the same time, the pension amounts of the retirees increase between 23% and 27% on average. This holds true for eight out of nine clusters. Moreover, the highest surplus is gained by clusters with discontinuous biographies. Thus, the risk of old-age poverty diminishes.

Finally, age-specific earning points emerge as a suitable instrument for the solution of all three parts of the second research question about the right incentive to foster employment at higher ages and the right reformation of the pension scheme in order to be flexible in regard to changes in the biography of future cohorts without losing sustainability.

6.2 Outlook

The current young working generation, which generates the pensions for the current retirees, is named generation Y and has several unique characteristics: highly motivated, internet savvy, provided with soft skills and international experiences. They grew up in a society with a lot of choices and possibilities. All these conditions foster individualism. An ecological way of life and a work-life balance are essential for this generation. This changes the labor supply and means that the demand has to be adapted accordingly, meaning flexible working hours, innovative working equipment, a minimum level of responsibility and autonomy, etc.[201]

Although the following generations might have other priorities again, a more flexible pension scheme is necessary to cover labor market developments and future careers, while providing adequate pension benefits to the elderly. It seems reasonable as a retiree with a complete employment biography to expect a pension benefit above the poverty level. Certainly, the public pension on its own should not be obligated to provide sufficient benefits but be a reliable part of the old-age income.

Moreover, threatening old-age poverty, related to the current pension system design and its restrictive reformations, is overestimated as the result of my analysis has shown. In the German pension scheme the pension payments are strongly linked to the employment career. The insurants collect earning points, which depend on the individual and average income level, during their working years. At the time of retirement the sum of earning points is calculated with the retirement formula into a monthly gross pension payment.[202] Earlier research has shown that a continuous as well as a long as possible employment career is crucial for a high amount of earning points.[203] The results of my analysis in chapter 5 confirm these findings. Discontinuous employment as well as a late labor market entry lead finally to a lower sum of earning points on average. Converted into pension payments, it means for the affected individuals a pension level below the poverty level on average. For a single household

[201] See Parment (2009).

[202] For a detailed explanation of the German pension scheme refer to section 5.2.

[203] See e.g. Riedmüller and Willert (2008) and Trischler and Kistler (2011).

this level is set by the government at 952€ per month.[204] Obviously, missing employment periods due to parenting, unemployment, care of family members and long education periods, lead to low amounts of earning points, and thus, to low pension payments as well. Therefore, individuals with a low income level, discontinuous employment careers and single mothers without employment face the risk of old-age poverty. These individuals were already affected by poverty during their working life and maybe even during their childhood. Gaps in education and a limited or even a lack of access to the labor market are the reasons behind that. So, in order to combat old-age poverty in the future, not the pension system design primarily, but the best possible education, starting as early as possible, is a relevant factor. Further, single mothers should be able to rely on a nationwide childcare supply, as well as on the flexibility and capacity of the labor market, in order to take up an employment.[205]

Although some statistics indicate an increase in old-age poverty, evidence for a relation to poverty starting already in younger years can be found too in most cases. Besides, it is remarkable, that the living standards of retirees and civil servant pensioners differ substantially and will not converge in the near future. This distributive inequality should receive more attention in the political and the social discussion.[206]

Innovative approaches may arise that today still sound utopian. So, the aging population might be an opportunity for the advancement of redistribution of work. So far, through taxes, subsidies and other forms of financial transfers, financial redistribution is taking place. In future, it could be an option to redistribute work, by reducing working hours in earlier as well as in later years. Older people would stay longer in employment gaining all positive effects like social inclusion and better well-being, while younger people would get the opportunity to focus on the family. Therefore, it might even lead to a rise in the birth rates.[207] Relevant research is needed for better knowledge and for recommendations about such pioneering concepts.

---

[204] See BMAS (2013)

[205] See Lewicki and Wigger (2013).

[206] See Noll and Weick (2012).

[207] See Vaupel and Loichinger (2006).

A similar provocative suggestion would be the concept of a European retirement scheme. Analyses and comparisons of national retirement schemes are various and regularly updated (e.g. studies of the European Commission or studies of the OECD). A uniform, European-wide pension system has not been discussed so far, neither in the academia nor in politics. With the joining of Croatia in 2013, the European Union consists of 28 member states, with about 506.8 Mio people.[208] One of the benefits of the European Union is the labor mobility across all member states. When exercising this right, no citizen should be discriminated against. Therefore, Regulation (EC) No 883/2004 was enacted, which regulates the coordination of social security systems. Although, the insured person is subjected to the legislation of a single member state only, the regulation ensures the principle of the aggregation of insurance periods as well as the neutrality of treatment. Insurance periods, employment periods and residence periods in one member state have to be considered in all other member states of the EU. More precisely, there are four basic principles of the recent coordination:

(1) Only the legislation of one single member state applies. There is no option to choose, but the social insurance agency decides about the responsibility.
(2) The same rights and duties apply, as for the citizen of the member state in which the insurance holds.
(3) Prior periods of insurance, employment or residence periods in other member states have to be credited in case of claiming benefits.
(4) Generally, monetary entitlements of one member state can be claimed from every other member state.

Besides this regulation on the coordination of social security systems, some other relevant harmonization has also occurred. The white paper *An Agenda for Adequate, Safe and Sustainable Pensions,* published in 2012 by the European Commission, is a document containing proposals for European Union action in this area. Further, the social protection committee (article 160 of the Treaty on the Function of the EU) is established by the council with the purpose to support the cooperation of the

---

[208] Own calculation based on preliminary statistics of Eurostat for 2012 (about 502.4 Mio (EU (27 member states) plus about 4.4 Mio (Croatia)).

commission and the member states within the field of social security. The committee has an advisory function, formulates opinions and prepares reports in the framework of the Open Method of Coordination.

Thus, in the field of retirement and pension system design further research is needed in order to be able to adapt to the developments in society in good time. Many countries with an aging society, including Germany, have already reacted with some reforms and changes concerning the pension scheme. As my thesis has revealed, not only demographic change, but also developments and changes on the labor market or in health conditions have a great impact on the pension and should be taken into account was well. Further, the pension system design also depends on global developments of the capital market as well as, in the case of Germany, on developments in the Eurozone. My thesis provides a deeper analysis of these relevant determinants and focuses on motives and incentives for a long-lasting employment. I provide a rather simple possibility of age-specific earning points to modify the current public pension scheme. In doing so, high incentives are provided to delay retirement instead of to retire early, as is still the case today. Automatically, the employment career is prolonged, leading to higher pension entitlements and therefore to a lower risk of old-age poverty.

Appendix

The appendix contains detailed statistics and evaluations from empirical research done in course of the thesis.

A.1 Results multiple logistic regression - chapter 4

Retirement[a]		Model 1		Model 2		Model 3	
		Signific.	Exp(B)	Signific.	Exp(B)	Signific.	Exp(B)
Early retirement	constant	,067		,048		,185	
	[gen=1]	,000	4,118	,000	4,864	,000	4,757
	[gen=2]	.	.	.	.	.	.
	[reg=1]	,000	1,941	,000	2,727	,000	3,868
	[reg=2]	.	.	.	.	.	.
	[edu=1]	,694	,816	,872	,910	,072	6,271
	[edu=2]	,562	1,346	,461	1,521	,014	12,084
	[edu=3]	,823	1,120	,710	1,233	,029	8,784
	[edu=4]	.	.	.	.	.	.
	[nchild=1]	,446	1,285	,984	1,008	,651	,722
	[nchild=2]	,062	1,682	,167	1,583	,889	1,090
	[nchild=3]	,249	1,359	,678	1,141	,643	,756
	[nchild=4]	,232	1,405	,245	1,487	,930	1,058
	[nchild=5]	,216	1,507	,372	1,432	,995	,996
	[nchild=6]	.	.	.	.	.	.
	[mart=1]	,602	1,203	,629	1,209	,651	,661
	[mart=2]	,754	,878	,971	,983	,175	,114
	[mart=3]	,428	,746	,412	,714	.	,939
	[mart=4]	.	.	.	.	.	.
	[ecosec=1]			,034	,532	,228	,556
	[ecosec=2]			,614	1,108	,189	,657
	[ecosec=3]			,511	,843	,184	,570

	[ecosec=4]			,604	1,105	,453	,784
	[ecosec=5]			.	.	.	.
	[comsiz=1]			,094	,580	,374	,604
	[comsiz=2]			,357	,780	,537	,762
	[comsiz=3]			,236	,748	,088	,522
	[comsiz=4]			,491	,826	,639	1,234
	[comsiz=5]			,051	,632	,045	,480
	[comsiz=6]			.	.	.	.
	[prof=2]			.	1,338	1,000	,666
	[prof=3]			,162	3,823	,995	3897944,156
	[prof=4]			,939	,951	,098	11,817
	[prof=6]			,033	,700	,003	,432
	[prof=7]			.	.	.	.
	[emp=1]			,329	,731	,727	,827
	[emp=2]			.	.	.	.
	[sbret=1]			,311	1,536	,402	1,780
	[sbret=2]			,005	4,237	,025	5,924
	[sbret=3]			,001	4,796	,004	8,261
	[sbret=4]			,210	1,796	,368	1,979
	[sbret=5]			,968	,981	,826	,843
	[sbret=6]			.	.	.	.
	[jint=1]			,278	1,289	,250	1,561
	[jint=2]			,011	2,080	,087	2,199
	[jint=3]			,334	1,352	,070	2,604
	[jint=4]			.	.	.	.
	[hincg=1]					,560	1,529
	[hincg=2]					,486	1,576
	[hincg=3]					,767	1,224
	[hincg=4]					.	.
	[asset=1]					,925	1,054
	[asset=2]					,349	,645
	[asset=3]					,964	1,021
	[asset=4]					.	.

	[save=1]					,292	,782
	[save=2]					.	.
	[open=1]					,481	,758
	[open=2]					,945	,979
	[open=3]					.	.
	[penhw=1]					,911	1,046
	[penhw=2]					,736	,888
	[penhw=3]					.	.
Deferred retirement	constant	,096		,655		,999	
	[gen=1]	,000	,160	,000	,290	,664	,753
	[gen=2]	.	.	.	.	.	.
	[reg=1]	,000	4,718	,000	2,699	,076	2,222
	[reg=2]	.	.	.	.	.	.
	[edu=1]	,088	3,430	,209	2,778	,980	746610,314
	[edu=2]	,208	2,451	,371	2,029	,981	600476,673
	[edu=3]	,342	1,953	,382	1,974	,980	689945,945
	[edu=4]	.	.	.	.	.	.
	[nchild=1]	,507	,755	,573	1,354	,534	,457
	[nchild=2]	,886	,949	,651	1,238	,792	,763
	[nchild=3]	,819	,924	,682	1,205	,563	,560
	[nchild=4]	,519	,784	,855	1,093	,384	,392
	[nchild=5]	,550	,766	,945	1,040	,720	,656
	[nchild=6]	.	.	.	.	.	.
	[mart=1]	,563	,795	,595	,786	,998	,000
	[mart=2]	,608	,786	,471	1,466	,998	,000
	[mart=3]	,439	,728	,376	,659	,998	,000
	[mart=4]	.	.	.	.	.	.
	[ecosec=1]			,277	,578	,400	,372
	[ecosec=2]			,727	1,110	,430	1,531
	[ecosec=3]			,730	,877	,969	1,029
	[ecosec=4]			,379	1,241	,409	1,496
	[ecosec=5]			.	.	.	.

[comsiz=1]			,885	1,067	,518	,586
[comsiz=2]			,285	1,516	,749	,803
[comsiz=3]			,622	1,203	,352	,552
[comsiz=4]			,268	1,597	,803	,831
[comsiz=5]			,901	1,048	,193	,435
[comsiz=6]			.	.	.	.
[prof=2]			.	############	,998	637522302,272
[prof=3]			,024	8,167	,994	158179425,917
[prof=4]			,995	,000	,987	,000
[prof=6]			,739	1,084	,862	1,089
[prof=7]			.	.	.	.
[emp=1]			,132	1,795	,318	2,095
[emp=2]			.	.	.	.
[sbret=1]			,000	,170	,009	,221
[sbret=2]			,000	,127	,181	,290
[sbret=3]			,000	,106	,038	,177
[sbret=4]			,000	,128	,110	,266
[sbret=5]			,000	,150	,019	,056
[sbret=6]			.	.	.	.
[jint=1]			,591	1,148	,266	1,718
[jint=2]			,228	1,514	,627	1,390
[jint=3]			,823	1,090	,796	1,234
[jint=4]			.	.	.	.
[hincg=1]					,219	,255
[hincg=2]					,658	,671
[hincg=3]					,780	,775
[hincg=4]					.	.
[asset=1]					,471	,524
[asset=2]					,226	,420
[asset=3]					,217	,436
[asset=4]					.	.
[save=1]					,184	,594

	[save=2]					.	.
	[open=1]					,048	4,586
	[open=2]					,789	1,207
	[open=3]					.	.
	[penhw=1]					,055	,307
	[penhw=2]					,017	,332
	[penhw=3]					.	.

a. The reference category is: regular retirement.

Nargelkerke-R^2: Model 1: 0,330; Model 2: 0,448; Model 3: 0,511

Classification Model 1

Observed	Predicted			
	Early retirement	Regular retirement	Deferred retirement	Percent correct
Early retirement	805	103	112	78,9%
Regular retirement	269	192	118	33,2%
Deferred retirement	49	58	225	67,8%
Overall percent	58,2%	18,3%	23,6%	63,3%

Classification Model 2

Observed	Predicted			
	Early retirement	Regular retirement	Deferred retirement	Percent correct
Early retirement	698	98	31	84,4%
Regular retirement	211	212	36	46,2%
Deferred retirement	52	70	125	50,6%
Overall percent	62,7%	24,8%	12,5%	67,5%

Classification Model 3

Observed	Predicted			
	Early retirement	Regular retirement	Deferred retirement	Percent correct
Early retirement	332	40	10	86,9%
Regular retirement	87	93	11	48,7%
Deferred retirement	21	16	42	53,2%
Overall percent	67,5%	22,9%	9,7%	71,6%

Bibliography

Aliyu, M. et al. (2008), *Alcohol consumption during pregnancy and the risk of early stillbirth among singletons*, Alcohol, Vol. 42, pp. 369–374.

Allianz Global Investors (2011a), *2011 Pension Sustainability Index*, International Pension Papers, No. 4/2011.

Allianz Global Investors (2011b), *Pension Systems in a Demographic Transition.*

Allianz Global Investors (2011c), *Project M – Global Pension Atlas 2011.*

Antolin, P. and Scarpetta, S. (1998), *Microeconometric Analysis of the Retirement Decision: Germany*, Economics Department Working Paper No. 204.

Arnds, P. and Bonin, H. (2002), *Frühverrentung in Deutschland: Ökonomische Anreize und institutionelle Strukturen*, IZA Discussion Paper No. 666.

Astleithner, F. et al. (2010), *Zur Entwicklung des Zugangsalters in Altersrenten verschiedener Qualifikationsgruppen in Deutschland (2003–2009)*, Deutsche Rentenversicherung 4/2010, pp. 539–564.

Atkinson, A. and Marlier, E. eds. (2010), *Income and living conditions in Europe*, Eurostat statistical books.

Backhaus, K. (2011), *Multivariate Analysemethoden : eine anwendungsorientierte Einführung*, 13th edition.

Bäcker, G. (2012), *Erwerbsminderungsrenten: Strukturen, Trends und aktuelle Probleme*, Altersübergangs-Report 2012-03.

Bäcker, G. et al. (2009), *Ältere Arbeitnehmer*, Erwerbstätigkeit und soziale Sicherheit im Alter, VS Verlag für Sozialwissenschaften.

Bakker, R. at al. (2010), *Associations of light and moderate maternal alcohol consumption with fetal growth characteristics in different periods of pregnancy: the Generation R Study*, International Journal of Epidemiology, Vol. 39, No. 3, pp. 777–789.

Becker, R. (1998), *Bildung und Lebenserwartung in Deutschland*, Zeitschrift für Soziologie, Vol. 27, No. 2, pp. 133–150.

Behrens, J. and Voges, W. (1996), *Kritische Übergänge: Statuspassagen und sozialpolitische Institutionalisierungen*, Schriften des Zentrums für Sozialpolitik, Vol. 4.

Bellmann, L. et al. (2007), *Demographischer Wandel: Betriebe müssen sich auf alternde Belegschaften einstellen*, IAB-Kurzbericht 21/2007.

Benartzi, S. and Thaler, R. (2004), *Save More Tomorrow: Using Behavioral Economics to Increase Employee Saving*, Journal of Political Economy, Vol. 112, No. 1, pp. S164–S187.

Van den Berg, G. et al. (2008), *Being Born Under Adverse Economic Conditions Leads to a Higher Cardiovascular Mortality Rate Later in Life: Evidence Based on Individuals Born at Different Stages of the Business Cycle*, IZA DP No. 3635.

Berkel, B. and Börsch-Supan, A. (2004), *Pension Reform in Germany: The Impact on Retirement Decisions*, MEA Discussion Paper 62–2004.

Berkel, B. and Börsch-Supan, A. (2006), *Auswirkungen verschiedener Reformszenarien auf Renteneintrittsentscheidungen*, Deutsche Rentenversicherung Bund, Forschungsrelevante Daten der Rentenverssicherung, DRV-Schriften, Band 55/2005, pp. 213–225.

Berlin (1884), *Der Reichskanzler und die Deutsche freisinnige Partei: Die Reden des Fürsten Bismarck und die Antwort des Abgeordneten Eugen Richter in der Reichstagssitzung vom 9. Mai 1884.*

Blomquist, S. and Luca Micheletto (2008), *Age related optimal income taxation, Scandinavian Journal of Economics*, Vol. 110, pp. 45–71.

Börsch-Supan, A. and Gasche, M. (2010), *Kann die Riester-Rente die Rentenlücke in der gesetzlichen Rente schließen?*, MEA Discussion Papers 201–2010.

Börsch-Supan, A. (2009), *50plus in Deutschland und Europa: Ergebnisse des survey of health, ageing and retirement in Europe*, VS Verlag.

Börsch-Supan, A. and Jürges, H. (2007), *Early Retirement, Social Security and Well-Being in Germany.*

Börsch-Supan A. (2004), *Faire Abschläge in der gesetzlichen Rentenversicherung,* Mannheimer Forschungsinstitut Ökonomie und Demographischer Wandel, Working Paper 65.

Bongaarts, J. and Feeney, G. (1998). *On the quantum and tempo of fertility.* Population and Development Review, Vol. 24, No. 2, pp. 271–291.

Bosch, G. (2012), *Prekäre Beschäftigung und Neuordnung am Arbeitsmarkt*, IGM Expertise, IAB.

Braun, R (2011), *Erben in Deutschland*, Wirtschatsdienst, Vol. 91, No. 10, pp. 724–726.

Brenke, K. (2013), *Immer mehr Menschen im Rentenalter sind berufstätig*, DIW Wochenbericht, No. 6.

Breyer, F. (2013), *Gesetzliche Rente: Bedeutet Teilhabeäquivalenz Verteilungsneutralität? – Ein weiterer Irrtum*, Wirtschaftsdienst, Vol. 93, No. 2, pp. 117–119.

Breyer, F. and Hupfeld, S. (2009a), *On the Fairness of Early-Retirement Provisions*, German Economic Review, Vol. 11, No. 1, pp. 60–77.

Breyer, F. and Hupfeld, S. (2009b), *Neue Rentenformel – mehr Gerechtigkeit und weniger Altersarmut*, DIW-Wochenbericht, Vol. 76, No. 5, pp. 82–86.

Breyer, F. and Hupfeld, S. (2009c), *Fairness of Public Pensions and Old-Age Poverty,* FinanzArchiv, Vol. 65, pp. 358–380.

Brockmann, H. and Klein, T. (2004), *Love and Death in Germany: The Marital Biography and its Effect on Mortality*, Journal of Marriage and Family, Vol. 66, No. 3, pp. 567–581.

Brønnum-Hansen H, Juel K. (2001), *Abstention from smoking extends life and compresses morbidity: a population based study of health expectancy among smokers and never smokers in Denmark*, Tobacco Control, Vol. 10, No. 3, pp. 273–278.

Brussig, M. (2011a), *Neueinstellungen im Alter: Tragen sie zu verlängerten Erwerbsbiografien bei?*, Altersübergangs-Report 2011–03.

Brussig, M. (2011b), *Weitere Zunahme der sozialversicherungspflichtigen Beschäftigung ab 50 Jahren*, Altersübergangs-Report 2011–02.

Brussig, M. (2010a), *Fast die Hälfte aller neuen Altersrenten mit Abschlägen – Quote weiterhin steigend*, Altersübergangs-Report 2010–01.

Brussig, M. (2010b), *Anhaltende Ungleichheiten in der Erwerbsbeteiligung Älterer; Zunahme an Teilzeitbeschäftigung*, Altersübergangs-Report 2010–03.

Brussig, M. (2010c), *Höhere Alterserwerbsbeteiligung durch längere Erwerbsphasen*, Altersübergangs-Report 2010–04.

Brussig, M. (2010d), *Erwerbstätigkeit im Alter hängt vom Beruf ab*, Altersübergangs-Report 2010–05.

Brussig, M. and Stegmann, T. (2006), *Wer geht vorzeitig in Rente? Eine Analyse mit den Individualdaten des Versichertenrentenzugangs 2004*, DRV-Schriften Band 55, pp. 135–157.

Budimir, K. (2007), *Inzidenz des vorzeitigen Rentenzugangs in Sozialsystemen mit versicherungsmathematischen Abschlägen*, DRV-Schriften Band 55/2007, pp. 43–66.

Büsch, V. et al. (2010), *Weiterbeschäftigung im Rentenalter*, BiB, Heft 129.

Bütler , M., et al. (2004), *What Triggers Early Retirement? Results from Swiss Pension Funds*, CEPR Discussion Paper No. 4394.

Bullinger, M. and Kirchberger, I. (1998), *Der SF-36-Fragebogen zum Gesundheitszustand. Handandweisung [SF-36-Questionnaire on health status]*, Hogrefe.

Bundesagentur für Arbeit (2012), *Der Arbeitsmarkt in Deutschland – Ältere am Arbeitsmarkt.*

Bundesministerium für Arbeit und Soziales (BMAS) (2013), *Lebenslagen in Deutschland – Der vierte Armuts- und Reichtumsbericht der Bundesregierung.*

Bundesministerium für Arbeit und Soziales (BMAS) (2012), *Verbreitung der Altersvorsorge 2011*, Forschungsbericht Sozialforschung 430, Endbericht.

Bundesministerium für Arbeit und Soziales (BMAS) (2010), *Aufbruch in die altersgerechte Arbeitswelt. Bericht der Bundesregierung gemäß § 154 Absatz 4 des Sechsten Buches Sozialgesetzbuch zur Anhebung der Regelaltersgrenze auf 67 Jahre.*

Bundesministerium für Arbeit und Soziales (BMAS) (2003), *Nachhaltigkeit in der Finanzierung der sozialen Sicherungssysteme*, Bericht der Kommission.

Bundesministerium für Bildung und Forschung (BMBF) (2013), *Weiterbildungsverhalten in Deutschland. AES 2012 Trendbericht.*

Bundesministerium für Familie, Senioren, Frauen und Jugend (BMFSJ) (2013), *Unternehmensmonitor Familienfreundlichkeit 2013.*

Bundesministerium für Familie, Senioren, Frauen und Jugend (BMFSJ) (2012), *Familienreport 2011.*

Bundesregierung (2012a), *Alterssicherungsbericht 2012.*

Bundesregierung (2012b), *Rentenversicherungsbericht 2012.*

Bundesregierung (2008), *Alterssicherungsbericht 2008.*

Case, A. and Paxson, C. (2005), *Sex differences in morbidity and mortality*, Demography, Vol. 42., No. 2, pp. 189–214.

Clemens, W. et al. (2007), *Beeinflusst die höchste schulische und berufliche Qualifikation das individuelle Rentenzugangsverhalten? – Eine empirische Analyse auf Datenbasis des Scientific Use Files Versichertenrentenzugang 2004*, Deutsche Rentenversicherung 7/2007, pp. 445–461.

Clemens, J. (2004), *Versicherungsmathematisch „faire" Abschläge bei vorzeitigem Renteneintritt*, Wirtschaftsdienst, Vol. 3, pp. 835–840.

Coppola, M. and Gasche, M. (2011), *Die Riester-Förderung – Mangelnde Information als Verbreitungshemmnis*, Wirtschaftsdienst, Vol. 91, No. 11, pp. 792–799.

Coppola, M. and Wilke, C. (2010), *How sensitive are subjective retirement expectations to increases in the statutory retirement age? The German case*, MEA discussion paper series.

Dathe, D. et al. (2011), *Monitor Engagement (Nr. 4) – Wie und wofür engagieren sich ältere Menschen?*, WZB.

Debrand T. and Sirven N. (2009), *What are the motivations of pathways to retirement in Europe: Individual, Familial, Professional Situation or Social Protection System?*, Working Paper, Institut de recherche et documentation en économie de la santé.

Deutsche Rentenversicherung Bund (2012), *Statistikband Rentenbestand am 31.12.2011*, Bd. 187.

Deutsche Rentenversicherung Bund (2011), *Rentenversicherung in Zeitreihen.*

Deutsche Rentenversicherung Bund (2010), *Deutsche Rentenversicherung in Zahlen 2010.*

Deutsche Rentenversicherung Bund (2008), *Rentenzugang 2007*, Statistik der Deutschen Rentenversicherung Band 168.

Diamond, P. (2005), *Social Security Rules that vary with age*, Pension systems - Beyond mandatory retirement, Forneo, E., Sestito, P. (eds.).

Dietz, M. and Walwei, U. (2011), *Germany – No Country for Old Workers?*, In: Zeitschrift für ArbeitsmarktForschung, Vol. 44, No. 4, pp. 363–376.

Dlugosz, S. (2011), *Clustering life trajectories*, Discussion Paper No. 11–015, Zentrum für Europäische Wirtschaftsforschung Mannheim.

Doblhammer, G. and Vaupel, J. (2001), *Lifespan depends on month of birth*, Proceedings of the National Academy of Sciences, Vol. 98, No. 5, pp. 2934–2939.

Eisenmenger, M. and Emmerling, D. (2011), *Amtliche Sterbetafeln und Entwicklung der Sterblichkeit*, Wirtschaft und Statistik 03/2011, p. 219 ff.

Erosa, A. and Gervais, M. (2002), *Optimal taxation in life-cycle economies*, Journal of Economic Theory, Vol. 105, pp. 338–69.

European Commission (2012a), *General Report on the Activities of the European Union – 2011.*

European Commission (2012b), *An Agenda for Adequate, Safe and Sustainable Pensions*, White Paper.

European Commission (2012c), *Active Aging*, Special Eurobarometer 378.

European Commission (2009), *Pension schemes and pension projections in the EU-27 member States 2008-2060*, European Economy, Occasional Papers No. 56.

Fahrmeir, L. et al. (2009), *Regression – Modelle, Methoden und Anwendungen.*

Fehmel, T. (2011), *Zwischen Gesetz und Tarif. Altersübergänge als Gestaltungsaufgabe*, Informationsdienst Altersfragen, 04/2011, pp. 9–13.

Fehr, H. et al. (2010), *Pension Reform with Variable Retirement Age – A Simulation Analysis for Germany.*

Fenge, R. et al. (2002), *Second-best properties of implicit social security taxes: Theory and evidence*, CESifo Working Paper 743.

Fennell, L. and Stark, K. (2005), *Taxation over time*, UCLA School of Law: Law-Econ Research Paper, pp. 05–24.

Fields, G. and Mitchell, O. (1982), *Economic determinants of the optimal retirement age: An empirical investigation*, National Bureau of Economic Research Cambridge.

Fries, J. (1980), *Aging, natural death, and the compression of morbidity*, New England Journal of Medicine, Vol. 303, No. 3, pp. 130–135.

Gasche, M. and Rausch, J. (2012), Auswirkungen einer Versicherungspflicht der Selbstständigen in der Gesetzlichen Rentenversicherung, MEA Discussion Papers 263–2012.

Gasche, M. (2012a), *Alte und neue Wege zur Berechnung der Rentenabschläge*, MEA Discussion Paper 252–2012.

Gasche, M. (2012b), *Bonusrente statt Zuschussrente*, Wirtschaftsdienst, Vol. 9, pp. 605–612.

Gasche, M. and Krolage, C. (2011), *Gleitender Übergang in die Rente durch Flexibilisierung der Teilrente*, MEA Discussion Papers 243–11.

Gilliland, F. et al. (2001), *Effects of maternal smoking during pregnancy and environmental tobacco smoke on asthma and wheezing in children*, American Journal of Respiratory and Critical Care Medicine, . Vol. 163, No. 2, pp. 429–436.

Gruenberg, E. (1977), *The Failure of Success*, Milbank Memorial Fund Quarterly, Health and Society, Vol. 55, No. 1, pp. 3–24.

Gunzelmann, T. et al. (2006), *Die subjektive Gesundheit älterer Menschen im Spiegel des SF-36*, Zeitschrift für Gerontologie und Geriatrie, Vol. 39, pp. 109–119.

Hannigan, J. and Armant, D. (2000), *Alcohol in pregnancy and neonatal outcome, Seminars in Neonatology*, Vol. 5, No. 3, pp. 243–254.

Himmelreicher, R. et al. (2008), *Die ferne Lebenserwartung von Rentnern und Pensionären im Vergleich*, WSI Mitteilungen 05/2008.

Himmelreicher, R. et al. (2009), *Bildung und Übergang in den Ruhestand*, Kölner Zeitschrift für Soziologie und Sozialpsychologie, Vol. 61, No. 3, pp. 437–452.

Himmelreicher, R. and Stuchlik, A. (2008), *Entwicklung und Verteilung von Entgeltpunkten in der gesetzlichen Rentenversicherung*, Deutsche Rentenversicherung, Vol. 6, pp. 532–547.

Hoffmann, H. (2007), *Wege in den Ruhestand*, Deutsche Rentenversicherung 62, 4-5, pp. 298–320.

Holzmann, R. and Hinz, R. (2005), *Old-Age Income Support in the 21st Century: An International Perspective on Pension Systems and Reform*, World Bank.

Holzmann, R. (2012), *Global Pension System and Their Reform: Worldwide Drivers, Trends and Challenges*, Social Protection and Labor Discussion Paper No. 1213.

Hubert, M. (1998), *Deutschland im Wandel: Geschichte der deutschen Bevölkerung seit 1815*, Franz Steiner Verlag.

Hurd, M.D. (1990), *The Joint Retirement Decision of Husband and Wives*, Issues in the Economics of Aging, ed. by D. Wise, pp. 231–258.

IBM SPSS (2010a), *Statistics 19 Algorithms.*

IBM SPSS (2010b), *Statistics Base 19.*

Igl, G. (2000), *Zur Problematik der Altersgrenzen aus juristischer Perspektive,* Zeitschrift für Gerontologie und Geriatrie , Vol. 33, No. 1, pp. 57–70.

Ilmarinen, J. (2012), *Förderung des aktiven Alterns am Arbeitsplatz,* Europäische Agentur für Sicherheit und Gesundheitsschutz am Arbeitsplatz.

Ilmarinen, J. (2009), *Work ability – a comprehensive concept for occupational health research and prevention,* Scandinavian Journal of Work, Environment and Health, Vol. 35, No. 1, pp. 1–5.

Ilmarinen, J. (2007), *The Work Ability Index (WAI),* Occupational Medicine, Vol. 57, No. 2.

Ilmarinen, J. (2006), *Towards a longer worklife. Ageing and the quality of worklife in the European Union.*

International Social Security Association ISSA (2011), *Mbao Pension Plan: A case of the Retirement Benefits Authority,* Good Practices in Social Security.

IWD (2010), Informationsdienst des Instituts der deutschen Wirtschaft Köln, Vol. 36, No. 22., 3. Juni 2010, p. 3.

Joebges, H. et al. (2012), *Auf dem Weg in die Altersarmut,* IMK Report 73.

Kahneman, D. and Krueger, A. (2006), *Developments in the Measurement of Subjective Well-Being,* Journal of Economic Perspectives, Vol. 20, No. 1, pp. 3–24.

Kalben, B. (2000), *Why men die younger: causes of mortality differences by sex,* North American Actuarial Journal, Vol. 4, No. 4, pp. 83–111.

Kannisto, J. (2012), *Effective retirement age in the Finnish earnings-related pension scheme,* Statistical Report 02/2012.

Katz, S. et al. (1983), *Active life expectancy,* The New England Journal of Medicine, Vol. 309, No. 20, pp. 1218–1224.

Katz, S. et al. (1963), *Studies of illness in the aged. The Index of ADL: a standardized measure of biological and psychosocial function,* Journal of the American Medical Association, Vol. 185, No. 12, pp. 914–919.

Keese, M. et al (2006), *Live longer, work longer,* OECD.

Keller, B. and Seifert, H. (2011), *Atypische Beschäftigung und soziale Risiken -Entwicklung, Strukturen, Regulierung,* WISO direkt 11/2011.

KFW (2012), *Selbstständigkeit in Deutschland – Trends und Einflussfaktoren,* KFW Research Standpunkt, No. 15, 02/2012.

Kifmann, M. (2008), *Age-dependent Taxation and the Optimal Retirement Benefit Formula,* German Economic Review, Vol. 9, pp. 41–64.

Kingston, G. (2000), *Efficient Timing of Retirement,* Review of Economic Dynamics, 3, pp. 831–840.

Koch, A. et al. (2011), *Soloselbstständige in Deutschland,* WISO Diskurs, 02/2011.

Kohli, M. (2000), *Altersgrenzen als gesellschaftliches Regulativ individueller Lebenslaufgestaltung: ein Anachronismus?,* Zeitschrift für Gerontologie und Geriatrie , Vol. 33, No. 1, pp. 15–23.

Kohli, M. (1985), *Die Institutionalisierung des Lebenslaufs: Historische Befunde und theoretische Argumente,* Kölner Zeitschrift für Soziologie und Sozialpsychologie No. 37, pp. 1–29.

Konietzka, D. (2010), *Zeiten des Übergangs,* VS Verlag für Sozialwissenschaften.

Krumm, S. et al. (2012), *No time for compromises: Age as a moderator of the relation between needs–supply fit and job satisfaction*, European Journal of Work and Organizational Psychology, doi: 10.1080/1359432X.2012.676248.

Kröger, K. et al. (2011), *Empirische Forschungsvorhaben zur Alterssicherung*, RatSWD Working Paper Nr. 170.

Kroll, D. (2012), *Programm: Zukunft, Antworten auf den demographischen Wandel*, Wiesbaden.

Kroll, L. et al. (2008), *Entwicklung und Einflussgrößen der gesunden Lebenserwartung*, Serial of the research group Public Health, Wissenschaftszentrum Berlin für Sozialforschung (WZB).

Kroll, L. and Lampert, T. (2009), *Soziale Unterschiede in der Lebenserwartung*, Methoden — Daten — Analysen, Vol. 3, No. 1, pp. 3–30.

Kruse et al. (2010), Erhaltung der beruflichen Leistungskapazität und Motivation älterer Arbeitnehmerinnen und Arbeitnehmer, Institut für Gerontologie der Universität Heidelberg.

Lafortune, G. and Balestat, G. (2007), *Trends in Severe Disability Among Elderly People - Assessing the Evidence in 12 OECD Countries and the Future Implications*, OECD Health Working Papers, No. 26.

Lawton, M. and Brody, E. (1969), *Assessment of older people: Self-maintaining and instrumental activities of daily living*, Gerontologist, Vol. 9, pp. 179–186.

Leber, U. et al. (2013), *Altersspezifische Personalpolitik: Wie Betriebe auf die Alterung ihrer Belegschaften reagieren*, IAB-Kurzbericht, 13/2013.

Lee, R. and Carter, L. (1992), *Modeling and Forecasting U. S. Mortality*, Journal of the American Statistical Association, Vol. 87, No. 419, pp. 659–671.

Lee, R. (2000), *The Lee-Carter method for forecasting mortality, with various extensions and applications*, North American Actuarial Journal, Vol. 4, No. 1, pp. 80–93.

Leve, V. and Zimmer, B. (2011), *Weiterbildungsbeteiligung älterer Beschäftigter - Risiken und Chancen*, in: Potenziale für die Arbeitswelt nutzen. Wie Unternehmen und ältere Beschäftigte profitieren (eds. Bundesarbeitskreis Arbeit und Leben e.V.), pp. 20–25.

Lewicki, M. and Wigger, B. (2013) *Wer ist von Altersarmut bedroht?*, Wirtschaftsdienst, Vol. 93, No. 7, pp. 462–465.

Lozachmeur, J. (2006), *Optimal age-specific income taxation*, Journal of Public Economic Theory, Vol. 8, pp. 697–711.

Lund, T. and Villadsen, E. (2005), *Who retires early and why? Determinants of early retirement pension among Danish employees 57-62 years*, European Journal of Ageing, Vol. 2, No. 4, pp. 275–280.

Luy, M. (2011), *Ursachen der Geschlechterdifferenz in der Lebenserwartung. Erkenntnisse aus der Klosterstudie*, Swiss Medical Forum, Vol. 35, No. 11, pp. 580–583.

Luy, M. (2010), *Tempo Effects and their Relevance in Demographic Analysis*, Comparative Population Studies – Zeitschrift für Bevölkerungswissenschaft, Vol. 35, No. 3, pp. 415–446.

Manton, K. (1982), *Changing concepts of morbidity and mortality in the elderly population*, Milbank Memorial Fund Quarterly, Vol. 2, Nr. 2, pp. 183–244.

Mathers, C. and Robine, J. (1997), *How good is Sullivan's method for monitoring changes in population health expectancies?*, Journal of Epidemiology and Community Health, Vol. 51, No. 1, pp. 80–86.

Mathers, C. (2002), *Health expectancies: An overview and critical appraisal*, in: Summary measures of population health: concepts, ethics, measurement and applications (eds. C. J. Murray, C. et al.), pp. 177–204.

Maxin, L. and Deller, J. (2010), *Beschäftigung statt Ruhestand: Individuelles Erleben von Silver Work*, Comparative Population Studies – Zeitschrift für Bevölkerungswissenschaft, Vol. 35. , No. 4, pp. 767–800.

McFadden, D. (1973), *Conditional logit analysis of qualitative choice behavior*, Frontiers in Econometrics.

Melbourne Centre for Financial Studies and Mercer (2012), *Melbourne Mercer Global Pension Index.*

Micheel, F. and Panova, R. (2013), *Entwicklung der Erwerbstätigkeit Älterer in Deutschland – Rückblick auf die letzten zwei Jahrzehnte*, Bevölkerungsforschung Aktuell 01/2013, pp. 6–12.

Montalto, C. P. et al. (2000), *Determinants of planned retirement age*, Financial Services Review, 9(1), p. 1-15.

Mueller, U. and Heinzel-Gutenbrunner, M. (2001), *Krankheiten und Beschwerden (subjektive Gesundheit) unter Bewertung der eigenen Gesundheit*, Datenanalyse für das Bundesinstitut für Bevölkerungsforschung, BIB Nachrichten, Issue 102c.

Mümken, S. and Brussig, M. (2013), *Die Arbeitsmarktpolitik wendet sich den Älteren zu*, Altersübergangs-Report, 2013–02.

Murray, C. et al. (2000), *A critical examination of summary measures of population health*, Bulletin of the World Health Organization, Vol. 78, No. 8, pp. 981–994.

Naegele, G. and Walker, A. (2006), *A guide to good practice in age management*, Office for Official Publications of the European Communities.

Noll, H. and Weick, S. (2012), *Altersarmut: Tendenz steigend*, Informationsdienst Soziale Indikatoren, Vol. 47, pp. 1–7.

OECD (2012a), *Pension Outlook 2012.*

OECD (2012b), *OECD thematic follow-up review of policies to improve labour market prospects for older workers.*

OECD (2011) *Pension at a Glance 2011.*

OECD (2009) *Pension at a Glance 2009.*

Oeppen, J. and Vaupel, J. (2002), *Broken Limits to Life Expectancy*, Science, Vol. 296, pp. 1029–1031.

Ohsmann, S. et al. (2003), *Rentenabschläge bei vorgezogenem Rentenbeginn: Welche Abschlagssätze sind 'richtig'?*, Deutsche Angestelltenversicherung, Vol. 4, pp. 1–9.

Oksuzyan, A. et al. (2008), *Men: good health and high mortality. Sex differences in health and aging.* Aging Clinical and Experimental Research, Vol. 20, No. 2, pp. 91–102.

Parment, A. (2009), *Die Generation Y - Mitarbeiter der Zukunft*, Gabler Verlag.

Piekkola, H. and Deschryvere, M. (2005), *Option Values for Retirement*, ENEPRI Research Report Nr. 14.

Pozzebon, S. and Mitchell, O. (1989), *Married women's retirement behavior*, Journal of Population Economics, Vol. 2, No. 1, pp. 39–53.

Promberger, M. et al. (2012), *Private Altersvorsorge fehlt, wo sie am nötigsten ist*, IAB Kurzbericht, 15/2012.

Queisser, M. and Whitehouse, E. (2006), *Neutral or Fair?: Actuarial Concepts and Pension-System Design*, OECD Social, Employment and Migration Working Papers 40.

Radl, J. (2007), *Individuelle Determinanten des Renteneintrittsalters*, Zeitschrift für Soziologie, Vol. 36, No. 1.

Radl, J. (2006), *Pfade in den Ruhestand und die Heterogenität des Renteneintrittalters – Eine Analyse auf Datenbasis des Scientific Use Files Versichertenrentenzugang 2004 des Forschungsdatenzentrums der Rentenversicherung*, Deutsche Rentenversicherung 9-10/2006, pp. 641-660.

Reil-Held, A. (2000), *Einkommen und Sterblichkeit in Deutschland: Leben Reiche länger?*, DP 00–14.

Reimers, C. et al. (2012), *Does Physical Activity Increase Life Expectancy? A Review of the Literature*, Journal of Aging Research, Vol. 2012.

Riedmüller, B. and Willert, M. (2008), *Die Zukunft der Alterssicherung, Analyse und Dokumentation der Datengrundlagen aktueller Rentenpolitik*, Gutachten um Auftrag der Hans Böckler Stiftung.

Riley, M. et al. (1999), *The aging and society paradigm*, in: Handbook of theories of aging, p. 327.

Riphahn, R. T. and Schmidt, P. (1995), *Determinanten des Rentenzugangs: Lockt der Ruhestand oder drängt der Arbeitsmarkt?,* MEA Discussion Paper, No. 10.

Robine, J. and Michel. J. (2004), *Looking Forward to a General Theory on Population Aging*, Journal of Gerontology: Medical Sciences, Vol. 59, No. 6, pp. 590–597.

Rogers, A. et al. (1989), *A multistate analysis of active life expectancy*, Public Health Report, Vol. 104, No. 3, pp. 222–226.

Ross, C. and Mirowsky, J. (2002), *Family Relationships, Social Support, and Subjective Life. Expectancy*, Journal of Health and Social Behavior, Vol. 43, No. 4, pp. 496–489.

Rust, J. (1994), Structural Estimation of Markov Decision Processes, Handbook of Econometrics IV, pp. 3082-–3143.

Sachverständigenrat (2011), *Herausforderungen des demografischen Wandels*, Statistisches Bundesamt.

Sackmann, R. (2008), *Chancen und Risiken der Festlegung von Altersgrenze des Ruhestands*, Zeitschrift für Gerontologie und Geriatrie , Vol. 41, pp. 345–351.

Sadana, R. et al. (2002), *Comparative analyses of more than 50 household surveys on health status*, in: Summary measures of population health: concepts, ethics, measurement and applications (eds. C. J. Murray, C. et al.), pp. 369–386.

Scherbov, S. and Sanderson, W. (2010), *Negative Folgen der Alterung bislang überbewertet*, Demographische Forschung aus erster Hand, Vol. 7, No. 4., pp. 1–2.

Scholz, R. and Schulz, A. (2009), *Haben Arbeitslosigkeit und Arbeitsunfähigkeit einen Einfluss auf die Höhe der Lebenserwartung?,* Sozialwissenschaftlicher Fachinformationsdienst Bevölkerungsforschung, Vol. 1, pp. 9–22.

Schröder, C. (2011), Riester-Rente: Verbreitung, Mobilisierungseffekte und Renditen, WISO Diskurs, Nov. 2011.

Siegrist, J. et al. (2006), *Quality of work, well-being, and intended early retirement of older employees – baseline results from the SHARE Study*, European Journal of Public Health, Vol. 17, No. 1, pp. 62–68.

Statistische Ämter des Bundes und der Länder (2011), *Demografischer Wandel in Deutschland*, Heft 1.

Statistisches Bundesamt (2012a), *Periodensterbetafeln für Deutschland 1871/1881 bis 2008/2010.*

Statistisches Bundesamt (2012b), *Periodensterbetafeln für Deutschland 2009/2011.*

Statistisches Bundesamt (2012c), *Berechnung von Periodensterbetafeln für Deutschland 1871/81 bis 2009/2011.*

Statistisches Bundesamt (2012d), *Geburten in Deutschland*, Ausgabe 2012.

Statistisches Bundesamt (2012e), *Mikrozensus Bevölkerung und Erwerbstätigkeit Stand und Entwicklung der Erwerbstätigkeit in Deutschland 2011*, Fachserie 1 Reihe 4.1.1.

Statistisches Bundesamt (2011), *Ältere Menschen in Deutschland und der EU.*

Statistisches Bundesamt (2010), *Gesundheit – Todesursachen in Deutschland.*

Statistisches Bundesamt (2009), *Bevölkerung Deutschlands bis 2060 - 12. koordinierte Bevölkerungsvorausberechnung.*

Steiner, V. and Geyer, J. (2010), *Erwerbsbiografien und Alterseinkommen im demografischen Wandel – eine Mikrosimulationsstudie für Deutschland*, Politikberatung kompakt 55, DIW Berlin.

Sullivan, D. (1971), *A Single Index of Mortality and Morbidity*, HSMHA Health Reports, Vol. 86, No. 4, pp. 347–354.

Szinovacz, M. and Davey, A. (2005), *Predictors of Perceptions of Involuntary Retirement*, The Gerontologist 45/2005.

Tenhunen, S. (2010), *Employment and accrued pension rights among the elderly – a peek into the pension registers*, Finnish Centre for Pensions Working Papers 2010:1.

Trischler, F. and Kistler, E. (2011), *Gute Erwerbsbiographien – Arbeitspapier 4: Wandel im Erwerbsverlauf und Rentenanspruch.*

Trischler, F. and Kistler, E. (2010), *Gute Erwerbsbiographien – Arbeitspapier 1: Erwerbsverläufe im Wandel.*

Urban, D. (1993), *Logit-Analyse: statistische Verfahren zur Analyse von Modellen mit qualitativen Response-Variablen.*

Vaupel, J. and Loichinger, E. (2006), *Redistributing Work in Aging Europe*, Science, Vol. 312, pp. 1911–1912.

Waldron, I. (1985), *What do we know about causes of sex differences in mortality? A review of literature*, Population Bulletin of the United Nations, Vol. 18, pp. 59–76.

Werding, M. (2007), *Versicherungsmathematisch korrekte Rentenabschläge*, Ifo Schnelldienst 16/2007, pp. 19–32.

WHO (1946), *The WHO Constitution.*

Widmer, R., et al. (2003), *Bestandsaufnahme und Interaktionen institutioneller Regelungen beim Rentenantritt*, Forschungsbericht Nr. 9/03.

Wigger, B. (2002), *Public Pensions and Economic Growth*, Springer.

Wilmoth, J. (2000), *Demography of longevity: past, present, and future trends*, Experimental Gerontology, Vol. 35, pp. 1111–1129.

Wilmoth, J. et al. (1996), *The Oldest Man Ever? A Case Study of Exceptional Longevity,* The Gerontologist, Vol. 36, No. 6, pp. 783–788.

Wingerter, C. (2009), *Der Wandel der Erwerbsformen und seine Bedeutung für die Einkommenssituation Erwerbstätiger*, Wirtschaft und Statistik 11/2009, Statistisches Bundesamt.

Wirtschaftsfaktor Alter (2010), Qualität der Arbeit und empfundene Arbeitszufriedenheit bei älteren Beschäftigten in Korrelation zum Altersbild und Age Management im Unternehmen.

Wrede, M. (1999), *Pareto efficient pay-as-you-go pension systems with multiperiod lives*, Jahrbücher für Nationalökonomie und Statistik 219, pp. 494–503.

Wübbeke, Christina (2012), *Ältere Arbeitslose am Scheideweg zwischen Erwerbsleben und Ruhestand: Gründe für ihren Rückzug vom Arbeitsmarkt*, Journal for Labour Market Research, Online First, 20 p.

Zahn, Y. et al. (2009), *Bridge employment and retirees' health: a longitudinal investigation, Journal of occupational health psychology*, Vol. 14, No. 4, pp. 374–389.

Zimmerer, M. (2012), *Global Pension Atlas Country Extract Germany.*